AF885224

This Social Media Workbook and Planner Belongs to:

If found, contact me here:

Phone: ____________________
Email: ____________________
Address ____________________

Dedicated To

YOU and my clients

Copyright @ 2015-2016 Dwainia Grey

All rights reserved. No part of this book may be reproduced, stored, or transmitted in any form or by any means, including scanning, photocopying, recording, or other electronic or mechanical methods, without the prior written permission of the publisher, except in the case of brief quotations embodied in critical reviews and certain other noncommercial uses permitted by copyright law. For permission requests, email info@awesomebizonline.com subject line "Attention Permissions Coordinator"

Limit of liability/disclaimer of warranty: While the publisher and author have used their best efforts in preparing this workbook and planner, they make no representations or warranties with respect to accuracy or completeness of the contents of this document and specifically disclaim any implied warranties of merchantability or fitness for particular purpose. No warranty may be created or extended by sales representatives, promoters, or written sales materials.

The advice and strategies contained herein may not be suitable for your situation. You should consult with a professional where appropriate. Neither the publisher nor author shall be liable for any loss of profit or any other commercial damages, including but not limited to special, incidental, consequential, or other damages.

Permissions
Please feel free to take photos of this planner (or your use of it) for the purposes of review or social media sharing. Please do not photograph the whole planner.

Published by
GreyChild Communications
Toronto, ON

Social Media Workbook and Planner / Dwainia Grey
ISBN-13: 978-0994888822

ISBN-10: 0994888821

INTRODUCTION

WHAT IS THIS?

This is the **Social Media Workbook and Planner** that will help you succeed with Social Media for your Empowerpreneur business. The book is based on the training in Awesome Nation Engagement; it's a companion book as well as a standalone workbook and planner. The Workbook Section of the book helps you create a Social Media strategy for the year and clarify your Social Media goals and tactics (action steps). The Planner Section of the book helps you plan your monthly Social Media strategy and track your monthly actions and milestones to get a clear picture of your Social Media Return on Investment (ROI).

By having a plan you leverage your time, reach targets (people and goals), add automation and measure success.

HOW TO USE THIS WORKBOOK

The first part is the **Strategy Workbook** which includes worksheets and checklists for you to complete. This helps you develop the Social Media Marketing Plan and success strategy for the coming months.

1. Objective
2. Audience
3. Branding
4. Style Guide
5. Engagement in 15 Minutes
6. Do's and Don'ts
7. Planning
8. Social Media Content Ideas
9. 52 Weeks
10. Social Media Visual Ideas
11. Social Media Image Cheat Sheet
12. Social Media Website Integration
13. Promotion Tracker
14. Holiday Promotions
15. Influencers
16. Passwords
17. Advertising Tracker
18. Video Post Ideas
19. Social Media Post Idea List
20. Getting Started Cheat Sheet
21. Resources
22. Blog Stats
23. Social Media Yearly Stats
24. Editorial Calendar

The second section is the **Social Media Action Planner**:

1. Monthly Calendar
2. Monthly Posts Tracker
3. Facebook Strategy
4. Twitter Strategy
5. LinkedIn Strategy
6. Google+ Strategy
7. Pinterest Strategy
8. Instagram Strategy
9. YouTube Strategy
10. Social Media Campaign Manager
11. Monthly Success Tracker
12. Monthly Stats
13. To Do
14. Notes

The planner section helps you plan your Social Media posts and engagement for the next 12 months. Each month includes monthly planning tools as well as metrics trackers. At the end of each month review the month and start planning for the new month. It's very important to complete your success tracker as it helps you to duplicate success.

The downloadable PDF contains 62 pages and allows you to print pages as needed.

INTRODUCTION

SOCIAL MEDIA TODAY

What is the biggest challenge that you are facing right now with Social Media?

What do you plan to accomplish?

What have you done so far to get your Social Media campaign started?

How much time do you currently spend on Social Media a week?

Are you directing Social Media fans and followers to your email list?

Are you currently using any of the following social media platforms?

- ☐ Facebook
- ☐ Linkedin
- ☐ Twitter
- ☐ YouTube
- ☐ Pinterest
- ☐ Google+
- ☐ Instagram
- ☐ Other sites

Social Media
MARKETING
WORKBOOK

Objective

Objective Overall Social Media objective for the year.

Increase reach
Build your brand
Engage influencers and connectors
Increase customer loyalty
Drive people to events
Improve customer service
Generate leads and sales
Convert leads to sales

Short-term

Goal # 1 –

Deadline

Action Plan

Goal Met ☐ Yes ☐NO

Goal # 2 –

Deadline

Action Plan

Goal Met ☐ Yes ☐NO

Goal # 3 –

Deadline

Action Plan

Goal Met ☐ Yes ☐NO

Long-term

Goal –

Deadline

Action Plan

Goal Met ☐ Yes ☐NO

Objective

Montly Goal Setter

Set realistic achievable goals for each month.
Goals can be a number of posts or number of new followers to engagement. Make sure it's measurable.

January	February
Goal Met ☐ Yes ☐NO	Goal Met ☐ Yes ☐NO
March	April
Goal Met ☐ Yes ☐NO	Goal Met ☐ Yes ☐NO
May	June
Goal Met ☐ Yes ☐NO	Goal Met ☐ Yes ☐NO
July	August
Goal Met ☐ Yes ☐NO	Goal Met ☐ Yes ☐NO
September	October
Goal Met ☐ Yes ☐NO	Goal Met ☐ Yes ☐NO
November	December
Goal Met ☐ Yes ☐NO	Goal Met ☐ Yes ☐NO

Your Preferred Client / Target Audience

Your Preferred Client is NOT the only person you will work with.

Your preferred client IS the only kind of person you will spend your marketing time, marketing energy, and marketing dollars attracting to your business.

If you market for every one, you market to no one.

Who is Your Preferred Client?

The people you most want to work with.
The people who want, need and are willing to pay for what your business provides.

- Who already wants, needs and is willing to pay for what your service provides?
- Where do you have contacts?
- Who would be the easiest clients to get?
- What group of people are you most comfortable with?
- Can you find them?

Research How to Find Your Preferred Client
Go online and in addition to the web you can use:

- Surveys/Questionnaires/Polls
- Interviews
- Observation
- Focus Groups
- Industry/Association Reports
- Your competitors
- Current Client Perception

Know Your Client
Fill Out Your Audience Section

Your Preferred Client Avatar

- Create your Preferred Client Avatar.
- You will have a solid understanding of who your target audience is and understand what their needs, interests, and goals are. You will understand how important your branding efforts are in influencing people to buy

Who is Your Competition?

Many businesses fail because they do not consider their competition. You need to do proper research about your competitors, learn what makes you different, why the customers should choose you, and much more.

What differentiates you from your competition?

Notes

AUDIENCE

Your Audience

- ☐ Existing clients
- ☐ Prospective clients

Where are they hanging out:

- ☐ Facebook
- ☐ Twitter
- ☐ Pinterest
- ☐ Instagram
- ☐ Google+
- ☐
- ☐
- ☐

Who Are Your Competitors? – How Do They Use Social Media? – How Are You Different?

What Keeps Your Client up at Night

How Does Your Product / Service Solve the Problem?

List 3 Successes You Have Had – Think RESULTS

AUDIENCE

What Words or Phrases Do Your Clients Use to Describe the Problem?	What Words or Phrases Do Your Clients Use When They Are Looking for the Solution? (KEYWORD)

Your Avatar

Name (fictitious)

Gender:

Age:

Profession:

Marital and Family Status:

Associations:

Location (city, neighborhood, or zip):

Branding

In 3 sentences write down your backstory.

Your Why

Who Are You?

When people see your posts what message, and feelings, do you want to convey?

How will you add your voice?

List 3 or more hashtags that match your brand.

List 3 or more hashtags your preferred client uses.

List 3 or more unique to you hashtags

Branding

Branding is all about the image of you and your business. The concept not only includes style, colors and logos, but also the image of perceived quality. Branding is also about your business and how it's different from your competitors. The purpose of a brand is to also distinguish yourself from everyone else. You may offer the same services as the next person but how do you differ?

Branding builds trust; it motivates purchasing and builds loyalty.

Building a brand that represents you will enhance your confidence as an Empowerpreneur and it will do the same thing in the eyes of the client. It will show them that you are committed to delivering what you promise. Branding also offers consistency for your business. It gives direction to both you and clients, so you know what to expect.

Practice Authentic Marketing

Know Your Why - Why do you do what you do? What is the deeper meaning behind what you do?

Know Your Business - Give an overview of your business, how you got started, and what makes you thrive today.

Know Your Story – Who are you? – Tell your story.
How is your journey similar to your preferred client?
What adversity have you overcome that that your preferred client can relate to?
Your Manifesto
Your Voice - Use your voice to tell your story and your message. Your voice is the way only you can express yourself and your unique view of the world. It shows your style, passion and beliefs

☐ Is your profile and cover image the same on all platforms?

☐ Is your profile picture and cover image of good quality and represent your brand?

☐ Does your description on each platform have the same message?

LOGO	PROFILE IMAGE

Style Guide

Image Text 1

Font
Size
Style
Color
Hex
RGB
CMYK

Image Text 2

Font
Size
Style
Color
Hex
RGB
CMYK

Watermark Text 1

Font
Size
Style
Color
Hex
RGB
CMYK

Image / Mascot

Insert Post Example

Show placement of watermark, text alignment, borders, etc.

Notes

Notes

Engagement

Are you interacting with followers, potential followers, and influencers?
Focus on your top 3 social media platforms daily.

Follow Influencers

- ☐ Create a list.
- ☐ Add their blogs to your Feedly.
- ☐ Add them to your favorites in Facebook, private list in Twitter.
- ☐ Make a note of Hashtags they use.
- ☐ Engage on their social media.
- ☐ Share, comment, like, retweet, +1

Social Media in 15 Minutes a Day

Engagement
Share / Retweet / Repin
Like (people in your network, influencers and clients)
Comment / Reply

Status update if applicable
Notifications
Respond to any comments via private message, or comments on posts
Acknowledge any new followers, likes and comments
Thank and reply

Share Content

Become a trusted resource.

Only share valuable content.

Share content that is useful to your fans and followers.

Share content that expresses your personality.

Spend 30 minutes to 1 hour each week filling up your scheduler. Use Feedly in conjunction with:

1. Platform specific scheduler (ex. Facebook Scheduler)
2. Tweetdeck
3. Hootsuite
4. BufferApp
5. Coschedule

Community Engagement

Participate in one Twitter Chat a week List 3 Twitter Chats to find your target market	Daily / Weekly focus on a Facebook group List 3 Facebook Groups to find your target market
Participate in one Google+ Hangout a week List 3 Hangouts to find your target market	Participate in a Pinterest Group Board List 3 Pinterest Group Boards to expand your reach

Social Media Do's and Don'ts

- ☐ Always follow the rules and regulations for each social media platform. If you don't, you can get your account suspended.
- ☐ Do create a social media marketing plan, but adjust your specific tactics as you go. Be flexible and take the time to find out what works and what doesn't work.
- ☐ Do commit the time and effort to maintain your social media marketing plan.
- ☐ Do pay attention to social media ethics.
- ☐ Do listen to your clients through your social media and respond where appropriate.
- ☐ Do participate – Join the conversation.
- ☐ Do pay attention to the metrics and analytics of your campaign.
- ☐ Do pay attention to trends. Be prepared to change your campaign to match the most recent trends.
- ☐ Do prepare to deal with how online users change, alter, or use your brand's message. Have a plan for both good and bad customer feedback.
- ☐ Do support promotional campaigns of your fans.
- ☐ Do support the promotional campaigns of other non-competitive businesses on your social media sites in exchange for their support.
- ☐ Don't forget to add attribution when it's not your content.
- ☐ Don't just post your own content.
- ☐ Don't post photos that will embarrass or humiliate someone or are unflattering.
- ☐ Don't share every moment of your day.
- ☐ Don't be disrespectful, offensive, vulgar, or use language considered to be inflammatory.
- ☐ Don't be rude or difficult to deal with when engaging with your fans.
- ☐ Don't lie to your clients or hide the fact that you are advertising to them. Always be transparent with your intentions.
- ☐ Don't overdo it when promoting your business. You want to use social media to build relationships, not overwhelm people with ads.
- ☐ Don't spam!

NOTES

Day-to-Day Management

How far ahead do you want to plan content?

How often will you promote your own content (blog posts, events, and products and services) versus other people's content?

What type of content are you going to share? Review the Post Idea Sheet. What you share needs to bring value - always think "What's in it for me?" Try for a combination of educating, and engaging. You are aiming to get them interested in you, your brand, and your business.

Who will create content? Images / Video / Copy

Who will post content?

Who will manage your Social Media campaigns?

Who will track, monitor, and report?

	Facebook	Twitter	Google+	LinkedIn	Pinterest	Instagram	YouTube	Other
Which social platforms will you use? Relevant to your business, and preferred client.								
How many times a week will you post on social media?								
What days and times will you post?								
Suggested number of times a week to post	2 daily	Hourly	Daily 3-5x week	Daily Min. 3x	5x daily	1-2 daily	1x week	

Planning

Do you want to assign posts to certain days a week? Throwback Thursday, Follow Friday, or make up your own

	Themed Post	Create Content	Publish Content
Monday			
Tuesday			
Wednesday			
Thursday			
Friday			
Saturday			
Sunday			

Resources

- ☐ Experienced Writer
- ☐ Professional Photos / Photo shoot
- ☐ Professional Videos / Video shoot
- ☐ Branded Graphics

Social Media Policy

Develop your Social Media Policy.

Read the Do's and Don'ts of Social Media. What are the policies you will have for your Empowerpreneur business?

- Rules of engagement
- How to handle customer service
- What to say and what not to say
- Workflow / Schedule
- How to handle negative feedback /criticism
    - Clients, media or competitors

Budget

Startup and launch budget
Campaign budgets
Ongoing management budget
- Advertising
- Design
- Tools (Canva, Pic Monkey, Hootsuite, Buffer, etc)

Metrics

Review your online metrics on a weekly and/or monthly basis. Use Google Analytics in conjunction with bitly, and the social media platform analytics to track and monitor your success. Also use Buffer and Hootsuite reporting tools.

Learn more about your return on investment (ROI – time and money) as well as which posts brings the most traffic, engagement and conversion.

Take time to complete the Blog Stats, Monthly Success Tracker and The Monthly and Yearly Social Media Tracker.

Download the weekly success tracker.
bit.ly/socialmarketingweekly

Va Va Voom

Value – 60% – Tips, tutorials, and instructional, useful, and helpful posts

List 3 topics that you can post about that will add value

Visual – 20% – Make use of images and videos

List 3 ways you can use images / videos in social media

Voice – 10% – Show your personality – personal posts about you, showing your life, and a behind the scenes view

List 3 posts that will show your personality

Marketing – 10% – Promotional posts to sell and promote your products and services

List 3 products / services you want to sell / promote via social media

Content Ideas for Social Media

1	**Valuable & Useful Information**	2	**Exclusive Promotions** Promotions to reward loyalty of fans and followers	3	**Contests** People really enjoy participating in contests, especially if they are easy to enter and have great prizes	4	**Host Live Events** Google+ Hangout, Facebook event or Twitter Chat
5	**Testimonials** Screen capture testimonials from other social media	6	**Call to Action**	7	**Blog Posts** Ensure every blog has a branded image	8	**Events, Workshops and Seminars** Share online and offline events you are hosting or attending
9	**Opt-in Offer** Free gift to build your mailing list	10	**Photos** Pictures of you and your products	11	**How to Tips**	12	**Business News** Updates about your business
13	**Quotes** Motivation and Inspiration	14	**Celebrate Holidays**	15	**Video** People love to watch videos	16	**Questions / Poll** Ask the community what they think
17	**Promotions** Promote your products, services, sales, and coupons	18	**Photo Caption** Get fans to come up with creative captions	19	**Lists / Top 10**	20	**Celebrate Milestones / Anniversaries** 100 fans, # of comments, etc. Reward for participation

Notes

52 Weeks

Plan out 52 weeks of Tips, Quotes, etc 52 Weeks of ______________________

1		27	
2		28	
3		29	
4		30	
5		31	
6		32	
7		33	
8		34	
9		35	
10		36	
11		37	
12		38	
13		39	
14		40	
15		41	
16		42	
17		43	
18		44	
19		45	
20		46	
21		47	
22		48	
23		49	
24		50	
25		51	
26		52	

Visual Ideas for Social Media

1	**Your Own Quotes**	2	**Events** Create a cover image and a sharable image for all your events	3	**Step by Step Instructions** Offer download or video	4	**Thursday Throwback** Can be of you or something that brings nostalgia
5	**Question** Use a photo to ask a question	6	**Selfies** Pics of yourself	7	**This or that** Show 2 options and solicit feedback	8	**Promotion** Every promotion must have an enticing image
9	**Fan Quote** Take a screenshot of a fan quote	10	**Product Shots** Pics of your products	11	**Blog Posts** Ensure every blog has a branded image	12	**Tip Sheet** Offer download or video
13	**Affirmation** Positive affirmations	14	**Customer Testimonial** Post a client testimonial or better yet, post a screenshot of a client testimonial	15	**Facts** People are fascinated with facts	16	**Famous / Favorite Quote** Quotes are very shareable
17	**Customer Photo** of you product	18	**How-to** Offer download or video	19	**Behind the scenes look**	20	**Infographic** Chock-full of useful information

MDG Advertising:

1. Content with images receives 94% more total views than content with just text.
2. 67% of customers consider detailed images to be more important than a list of the product description and customer ratings.
3. When making a buying decision, 60% of consumers are more likely to consider or contact a business if they see images about their products show up in search results.
4. Facebook's marketing statistics have shown us that businesses will see a 37% increase in engagement when their Facebook posts include photos or some type of graphics.

Social Media Image Cheat Sheet

Platform	Image Size
Facebook Profile Photo	180 x 180
Facebook Cover Photo	851 x 315
Facebook Post Photo	504 width x any length
Facebook Tab Photos (Apps)	111 x 74
Facebook Group	801 x 250
Facebook Event	785 x 295
Twitter Profile	400 x 400
Twitter Header	1500 x 500
Twitter Background	1280 x 1024
Twitter Shared Image	440 x 220
Google+ Profile	250 x 250
Google+ Cover	1080 x 608
Google+ Post	497 x 373
Pinterest Profile	165 x 165
Pinterest Board Cover	222 x 150
Pinterest Pin	735 x any length
Instagram Profile	110 x 110
Instagram	640 x 640
LinkedIn Profile Photo	200 x 200
LinkedIn Background (Profile)	1400 x 425
LinkedIn Company Logo	100 x 60
LinkedIn Company Banner	646 x 220
YouTube Channel	2560 x 1440
YouTube Thumbnail	1280 x 720

Social Media Post Ideas

Social Media Post Ideas	Image	Edited	Scheduled

Social Media Post Ideas

Social Media Post Ideas	Image	Edited	Scheduled

Social Media Post Ideas

Social Media Post Ideas	Image	Edited	Scheduled

Social Media Post Ideas

Social Media Post Ideas	Image	Edited	Scheduled

Video Post Ideas

Video Type	Video	Video Tags	Date	Time	

Promotion Tracker

Plan 1-3 promotions / campaigns for each month. Can be as simple as celebrating an event, or a call to action.

January		February	
Start Date:	End Date:	Start Date:	End Date:
March		April	
Start Date:	End Date:	Start Date:	End Date:
May		June	
Start Date:	End Date:	Start Date:	End Date:
July		August	
Start Date:	End Date:	Start Date:	End Date:
September		October	
Start Date:	End Date:	Start Date:	End Date:
November		December	
Start Date:	End Date:	Start Date:	End Date:

Holiday Promotion Ideas

Ideas	Holiday Event	

Advertising Tracker

Ad	Start	End	Cost	

Influencers

Name	Facebook	Twitter	Pinterest	Instagram	Blog

PASSWORDS

Website	Username	Email	Password

Website Integration

Website

☐ Add Facebook Share buttons to your website
Plugins for WordPress - Digg Digg, Jetpack, or Shareaholic

Social Media Profile Links

☐ Contact Page

☐ About Page

☐ Sidebar

☐ Footer

☐ Social Media Widget - Choose a Social Media Platform that you are most active on – does it fit your design?

Comment

☐ Enable commenting on your blog posts

☐ Check daily and respond to any comments
Plugins for WordPress – Disqus or Comment Luv

Blog

☐ Branded image with each post

☐ Call to action with each post

☐ Embed Facebook updates in posts

☐ Monitor and track your website using analytic tools such as Google Analytics

☐ Search Engine Optimize (SEO) all posts
Plugins for WordPress – Yoast SEO, All-in-One-SEO Pack, or SEO Ultimate

Getting Started Cheat Sheet

Branding

- [ ] I have a clear description of who my target audience is.
- [ ] I know what personality/ brand message and image I want to communicate.
- [ ] I've created a username that will be easy to find, follow, and connect with.
- [ ] I have the same profile username across social media platforms.
- [ ] I consistently use my branding (image, logo, tagline, etc…) in all online communication.
- [ ] I use a branded social media cover /header images.
- [ ] I've included contact information in my profiles including my URL.
- [ ] I have included a professional email address - @yourwebsite.com
- [ ] I have included my business location (where applicable - at least put country).
- [ ] I ensure I use the correct NAP (Name, Address and Phone number - where applicable).
- [ ] I've included a professional photo of myself.
- [ ] I have a complete about / bio section with links to my website
- [ ] I have linked and verified my website.
- [ ] I link to other social media profiles (where applicable).
- [ ] Each of my social media profiles is 100% complete.

Planning

- [ ] I have a *Social Media Marketing Plan* that I use to help guide my online marketing.
- [ ] I have defined my social media marketing goals and know how I will track them.
- [ ] I've created systems to test and track my social media marketing goals and tactics.
- [ ] I've integrated my social media marketing tactics into my overall marketing strategies.
- [ ] I've use relevant dashboards and automation tools such as Hootsuite to optimize my time.
- [ ] I've documented the systems and tools I use, so it can be easily delegated.
- [ ] I have created a posting schedule for the social media platforms I will be focusing on.

Getting Started Cheat Sheet

Content

- ☐ I've researched the best places to find content related to my topic and relevant to my target audience.
- ☐ I use the right tools to find, organize, and distribute content.
- ☐ I have developed a system to find valuable content to share.
- ☐ I make sure I share a good mix of content (*Va Va VooM* – Value, Voice, Visual, and Marketing).
- ☐ I'm creating specific promotions and offers for my social media audience - *EXCLUSIVE*.
- ☐ I use an editorial calendar to layout content for my blog, email newsletter, and social media posts.
- ☐ I follow the top blogs in my industry to stay on top of trends.
- ☐ I create content to share on all platforms – Facebook, LinkedIn, Twitter, Google+, Pinterest, and Instagram.
- ☐ I have at least 3 main #hashtags I use.
- ☐ I have made my website shareable with widgets and plugins.
- ☐ I always check for grammar and spelling.

Engagement

- ☐ I've researched the social media platforms to use to reach my target audience.
- ☐ I have started to connect and follow people – co-workers, employees, past and current clients, people I admire, people in my industry, and my competitors.
- ☐ I've invited my friends, associates, and clients to connect with me.
- ☐ I've joined the right groups, lists, and communities where my target audience hangout
- ☐ I participate in those groups by posting content, answering questions, and starting the conversation.
- ☐ I comment on relevant blogs in my industry/niche.
- ☐ I respond to comments posted to my blog.
- ☐ I create and participate in contests, events, and special online activities.
- ☐ I spend 15 minutes a day on engagement – I interact with my Awesome Nation – answer comments (good or bad), respond to messages, share, retweet, repin, like and promote other people's content.

Social Media Resources

Post Scheduling – BufferApp.com, Hootsuite.com, CoSchedule.com, PostPlanner

Image Design – Canva, PicMonkey, Pixlr, A Beautiful Mess App

Facebook Insights, Woobox, Pagemodo, Dlvr.it, NetworkedBlogs, Rafflecopter, Wishpond, Facebook Marketing Workbook and Planner

Twitter Analytics, Tweroid, Followonk, TweetDeck, Twitter Marketing Workbook and Planner

LinkedIn Insights, SlideShare.net, LinkedIn Marketing Workbook and Planner

Google+ Insights, Google+ Marketing Workbook and Planner

Ahalogy, Viraltag, BoardBooster, tailwindapp.com, gopixel.me, Pinterest Marketing Workbook and Planner

iconosquare.com, schedugr.am, latergram.me, AutoGrammer, VSCO, Pic Stitch, Photo Grid, Instagram Marketing Workbook and Planner

Blog Stats

	Date	Facebook	Twitter	Google+	Pinterest	Instagram	Blog Visits
1							
2							
3							
4							
5							
6							
7							
8							
9							
10							
11							
12							
13							
14							
15							
16							
17							
18							
19							
20							
21							
22							
23							
24							
25							
26							
27							
28							
29							
30							
31							
32							
33							
34							
35							
36							
37							
38							
39							
40							
41							
42							
43							
44							
45							
46							
47							
48							
49							
50							
51							
52							

Social Media Yearly Stats

Year	Facebook		Twitter		Pinterest		Instagram		Newsletter			
	Goal	Actual	Goal	Actual	Goal	Actual	Goal	Actual	Goal	Actual	Goal	Actual
January												
February												
March												
April												
May												
June												
July												
August												
September												
October												
November												
December												
Yearly Total												

EDITORIAL CALENDAR

Content Calendar

Create your content calendar with something simple like an online Google calendar, an Excel spreadsheet, a Word document, desk calendar or whatever you're comfortable with. Your content calendar should include your company's events, upcoming promotions or products your company plans to launch this year. This is not set in stone, be flexible and ready to make changes.

By planning ahead with dates you can refer back to, you will find your social media updates easier to manage.

Review your calendar, and for each week decide:

- ☐ What type of content you will post?
- ☐ What days of the weeks you will post your messages?
- ☐ Will you use an image or video for visuals?
- ☐ Indicate which social media network that you'll use with each blog post.

Here is a link to the Excel Calendar that I use.
bit.ly/socialmarketingweekly

Social Media
MARKETING
PLANNER

Editorial Calendar

Month

SUNDAY	MONDAY	TUESDAY	WEDNESDAY	THURSDAY	FRIDAY	SATURDAY

Notes

Acknowledge and Celebrate Your Success

Month:

Post with most engagement (shares, likes, and comments) on Facebook	Total Reach This Month
Most retweeted post on Twitter and number of retweets	Number of @Mentions
Most repined post on Pinterest and number of repins	Best Performing Board
Most loved Instagram photo this month and number of loves	Most Successful Hashtag
Most viewed video on YouTube and number of views	Number of videos uploaded this Month

This month I learned

A record I broke this month

My celebration this month

Next month I plan to do the same

Next month I plan to try (new)

Social Media Monthly Stats

FACEBOOK	Total Fans	New Fans	# of Posts	# of Likes	# of Comments	# of Clicks to Website
TWITTER	Total Followers	New Followers	# of Tweets	# of RT's	# of Favorites	# of Clicks to Website
GOOGLE+	Total Followers	New Followers	# of Posts	# of +1's	# of Comments	# of Clicks to Website
PINTEREST	Total Followers	New Followers	# of Pins	# of Repins	# of Likes	# of Clicks to Website
INSTAGRAM	Total Followers	New Followers	# of Pics	# of Comments/Likes		
LINKEDIN	Total Connections	New Connections	# of Posts	# of Comments/Likes		# of Clicks to Website
Other	Total Followers	New Followers	# of Posts	# of Engagement		# of Clicks to Website
EMAIL SUBSCRIBERS FROM SOCIAL MEDIA						

Social Media Posts

	Date	Posts	Post Scheduled	
Mon				
Tue				
Wed				
Thu				
Fri				
Sat				
Sun				
Mon				
Tue				
Wed				
Thu				
Fri				
Sat				
Sun				
Mon				
Tue				
Wed				
Thu				
Fri				
Sat				
Sun				
Mon				
Tue				
Wed				
Thu				
Fri				
Sat				
Sun				

Facebook

Post Ideas

- [ ] Post links, photos, events and video
- [ ] Share Blog Posts in Groups, Status Updates, and Facebook Page
- [ ] Share other's content
- [ ] Post Regularly (max 2 times a day on your page)

List Groups to Join / Start

- [ ] Add value
- [ ] Ask and respond to questions
- [ ] Post insightful comments
- [ ] Announce new members to your group

Facebook Tools

- [ ] Video – uploading video direct to Facebook gets more exposure
- [ ] Photo – create blog posts albums by category
- [ ] Apps / Tabs - Pinterest, Twitter, Instagram, email subscription etc.
- [ ] Facebook Workbook and Planner

Facebook Strategy

1. Is my preferred client using Facebook?
2. What is my objective?
3. Have I included a professional photo on my personal profile?
4. Do I have a completed Facebook Page with a logo, and branded cover?
5. About section includes keywords and URL - reflects my voice and brand.
6. Claim my custom Facebook URL.
7. Use insights to create targeted posts and know the best day and time for engagement.
8. I create super targeted ads with Facebook Advertising.
9. Integrate Facebook on my website

- [ ] Facebook Profile buttons
- [ ] Facebook Widget
- [ ] Facebook Share buttons
- [ ] Embed Facebook posts on blog posts

10. I have a (monthly/ weekly / daily) schedule for Facebook.
11. I have a (monthly/ weekly/ daily) Facebook engagement schedule.

- [ ] Post Status Updates and in groups
- [ ] Respond to all messages and comments on my page
- [ ] Tag people when I post their content
- [ ] Comment as my page

12. I have a strategy to capture leads from Facebook.
13. I have a strategy to get fans and friends to buy.
14. I always add value.
15. I am always connecting to:

- [ ] Influencers
- [ ] Current, Past and Future Clients
- [ ] Future Collaborators
- [ ] Family and Friends

Facebook Status Updates

Facebook Status Updates	Date	TIme	✓

Twitter

Post Ideas

☐ Post links, photos, and video

☐ Share Blog Posts in Groups, Status Updates and Twitter Page

☐ Share other's content

☐ Post Regularly

List Twitter Chats To Join / Start

☐ Add value

☐ Ask and respond to questions

☐ Post insightful comments

☐ Participate in niche, industry, and interests chats

Twitter Tools

☐ Lists – Create public and private lists

☐ Images and Video – Post branded photos and videos

☐ Twitter Cards – Add twitter cards to your website

☐ Twitter Workbook and Planner

Twitter Strategy

1. Is my preferred client using Twitter?
2. What is my objective?
3. Branded Bio, URL, profile image (professional photo or logo) profile header, and background image.
4. Link to other social media profiles
5. Always use #hashtags.
6. Use Twitter Analytics to create targeted posts.
7. Use Twitter Ads.
8. Integrate Twitter on my website

☐ Twitter Profile buttons

☐ Twitter Widget

☐ Twitter Share buttons

☐ Embed Twitter posts on blog posts and/or testimonials

☐ Use click to Tweet

9. Preface posts with comments
10. Periodically clean up my Twitter feed and unfollow spam and inactive accounts.
11. I have a (monthly/ weekly / daily) schedule for Twitter.
12. I have a (monthly/ weekly/ daily) Twitter engagement schedule.

☐ Update ☐ Retweet

☐ Respond ☐ Favorite

☐ Mention ☐ Direct Message

13. I have a strategy to capture leads from Twitter.
14. I have a strategy to get fans and friends to buy.
15. I always add value.
16. I am always connecting to:

☐ Influencers

☐ Current, Past and Future Clients

☐ Future Collaborators

☐ Family and Friends

Twitter Status Updates

Twitter Status Updates	Date	TIme	✓

LinkedIn

Post Ideas

☐ Utilize LinkedIn Posts

☐ Share Blog Posts in Groups, Status Updates, and Company Page

☐ Share other's content

☐ Links

☐ Post Regularly

List Groups to Join / Start

☐ Add value

☐ Ask and respond to questions

☐ Post insightful comments

LinkedIn Tools

☐ Projects – projects you have worked on and completed

☐ Publications – books, eBooks, workbooks, planners, etc., you have created

☐ Portfolio – showcase your work / creations

☐ LinkedIn Workbook and Planner

LinkedIn Strategy

1. Is my preferred client using LinkedIn?
2. What is my objective?
3. Have I included a professional photo?
4. Do I have a branded bio – my voice and brand?
5. Is my profile 100% complete?
6. Is my profile Search Engine Optimized?
7. My posts are compelling content and includes images
8. I have a (monthly/ weekly / daily) schedule for LinkedIn.
9. I have a (monthly/ weekly/ daily) LinkedIn engagement schedule.
   - ☐ Status Updates
   - ☐ Groups
   - ☐ Endorsements
   - ☐ Recommendations
10. I have a completed Company Page.
11. I have a strategy to capture leads from LinkedIn.
12. I have a strategy to get connections and followers to buy.
13. I always add value.
14. I am always connecting to:
    - ☐ Influencers
    - ☐ Current and Past Clients
    - ☐ Future Clients
    - ☐ Future Collaborators
    - ☐ Family and Friends

LinkedIn Status Updates

LinkedIn Status Updates	Date	TIme	✓

Google+

Post Ideas

- [ ] Post texts, links, photos, events, and video
- [ ] Share Blog Posts in Communities, Status Updates and Google+ Page
- [ ] Share other's content
- [ ] Post Regularly

List G+ Communities To Join / Start

- [ ] Add value
- [ ] Ask and respond to questions
- [ ] Post insightful comments at least once a week

Google+ Tools

- [ ] Create Targeted Circles – Influencers, clients, prospects and top engagers
- [ ] G+ Communities – Join communities and follow members
- [ ] Attend and Host G+ Hangouts – Live on air, webinar, panel discussion, video conference, video call, client meetings, screen share, etc
- [ ] Google+ Workbook and Planner

Google+ Strategy

1. Is my preferred client using Google+?
2. What is my objective?
3. Create a G+ profile page, and include professional photo.
4. Create a branded G+ Business Page (Description, Tagline, URL, logo, cover image, contact info, etc.).
5. Claim G+ authorship.
6. Claim your custom URL.
7. Share Google+ posts on other social media profiles.
8. Always use #hashtags.
9. Use keywords and descriptions.
10. Be consistent.
11. Vary posts – long and short
12. Use Google Analytics to create targeted posts.
13. Schedule posts.
14. Integrate Google+ on my website.

- [ ] Google+ Badge
- [ ] Google+ Profile buttons
- [ ] Google+ Share buttons

15. I have a (monthly/ weekly / daily) schedule for Google+.
16. I have a (monthly/ weekly/ daily) Google+ engagement schedule.

- [ ] +1
- [ ] Comment
- [ ] Mention (+ in front of name)
- [ ] Respond to mentions
- [ ] Thank people who share my content
- [ ] Tag people when I share their content

17. I have a strategy to capture leads from Google+.
18. I always add value.
19. I am always connecting to:

- [ ] Influencers
- [ ] Current, Past and Future Clients
- [ ] Future Collaborators
- [ ] Family and Friends

Google+ Status Updates

Google+ Status Updates	Date	TIme	✓

Pinterest

Post Ideas

- ☐ Share Blog Posts on multiple boards (ensure each blog post has a pinnable image and make more than one image per blog posts)
- ☐ Share other's content
- ☐ Post Regularly

List Group Boards to Join / Start

- ☐ Add value
- ☐ Post insightful comments

Pinterest Tools

- ☐ Boards – Organize and SEO your boards with optimized board names and descriptions
- ☐ Video – Pin branded videos
- ☐ Pinterest Workbook and Planner

Pinterest Strategy

1. Is my preferred client using Pinterest?
2. What is my objective?
3. Have a I included a professional photo or logo in my profile.
4. Get verified and claim your custom Pinterest URL.
5. Use quality images.
6. Schedule posts.
7. Use #hashtags.
8. Vary vertical and horizontal images.
9. Use Pinterest Analytics to see what images people are pinning.
10. Use Pinterest Advertising.
11. Integrate Pinterest on my website
    - ☐ Pinterest Profile buttons
    - ☐ PinIt button
    - ☐ Pinterest Widget
    - ☐ Pinterest Share buttons
    - ☐ Embed Pinterest boards and posts on blog posts.
12. I have a (monthly/ weekly / daily) schedule for Pinterest.
13. I have a (monthly/ weekly/ daily) Pinterest engagement schedule.
    - ☐ Follow users
    - ☐ Like
    - ☐ Repin
    - ☐ Respond to mentions
    - ☐ Tag others
    - ☐ Comment
14. I have a strategy to capture leads from Pinterest.
15. I have a strategy to get fans and friends to buy.
16. I always add value.
17. I am always connecting to:
    - ☐ Influencers
    - ☐ Current, Past and Future Clients
    - ☐ Future Collaborators
    - ☐ Family and Friends

Pinterest Status Updates

Pins	Date	TIme	✓

Instagram

Post Ideas

- ☐ Post quality images and video
- ☐ Share Blog Posts
- ☐ Share other's content
- ☐ Post Regularly (add at least one new image daily – 2x max)

List 20 Most Used HashTags For Your Niche / Industry

- ☐ Add value
- ☐ Post insightful comments

Instagram Tools

- ☐ Filters – Visual effects over images and videos
- ☐ Video – Upload 3-15 second video directly to Instagram
- ☐ Instagram Workbook and Planner

Instagram Strategy

1. Is my preferred client using Instagram?
2. What is my objective?
3. I have a professional photo or logo on my profile.
4. I have added contact info and URL to profile
5. I have included a keyword rich bio.
6. Use short, SEO descriptions on posts.
7. Add relevant #hashtags to posts.
8. Use #hashtags in comments.
9. Use custom #hashtags on promotions, products, etc.
10. Share Instagram posts on other social media.
11. I am personable, real and authentic.
12. Integrate Instagram on my website
    - ☐ Instagram Profile buttons
    - ☐ Instagram Widget
    - ☐ Embed Instagram posts on blog posts where applicable.
13. I have a (monthly/ weekly / daily) schedule for Instagram.
14. I have a (monthly/ weekly/ daily) Instagram engagement schedule.
    - ☐ Like
    - ☐ Comment
    - ☐ Tag people
    - ☐ Follow and follow back
    - ☐ Respond to comments
15. I have a strategy to capture leads from Instagram.
16. I have a strategy to get fans and friends to buy.
17. I always add value.
18. I am always connecting to:
    - ☐ Influencers and bloggers
    - ☐ Current, Past and Future Clients
    - ☐ Future Collaborators
    - ☐ Family and Friends
    - ☐ Brands

Instagram Status Updates

Instagram Updates	Date	TIme	✓

YouTube

Post Ideas

- ☐ Create a video editorial calendar
- ☐ Reviews, demos, tutorials, testimonials and commercials

List Channels to Subscribe / Start

- ☐ Add value
- ☐ Post insightful comments

YouTube Tools

- ☐ Playlists – Group services, tutorials, client resources, or theme categories
- ☐ G+ Hangouts – Create live broadcasts on YouTube

YouTube Strategy

1. What is my YouTube marketing objective?
2. I included a professional photo on my personal profile.
3. I have a completed YouTube Channel (Icon, Art, Description, Links and URL).
4. I have created branded preview image for each video.
5. I have created a branded video intro and outro.
6. Optimize each video (Keyword in Title, Description, and Tags)
7. Use playlists.
8. Use YouTube Analytics
9. Use annotations – text, links, and graphics placed over video
10. Link to other social media platforms.
11. Integrate YouTube on my website
    - ☐ YouTube Profile buttons
    - ☐ YouTube Widget
    - ☐ YouTube Share buttons
    - ☐ Embed YouTube posts on blog posts.
12. I have a (monthly/ weekly / daily) schedule for YouTube.
13. I have a (monthly/ weekly/ daily) YouTube engagement schedule.
    - ☐ Share videos on other social media channels.
    - ☐ Like, share and comment on others' videos.
    - ☐ Respond to comments.
    - ☐ Subscribe to others' YouTube Channels.
14. I have a strategy to capture leads from YouTube.
15. I have a strategy to get fans and friends to buy.
16. I always add value.
17. I am always connecting to:
    - ☐ Influencers
    - ☐ Current, Past and Future Clients
    - ☐ Future Collaborators
    - ☐ Family and Friends

Campaign Sheet

Product / Service Campaign

Campaign	
Description	
Product / Service Newsletter Contest / Giveaway	
Start	End
Objective	
Target Audience	
Budget$ / Cost$ / Return$	
Landing Page	
Tracking Link	
Days and Time	
Winner / Date Notified	

Image

- ☐ Blog Post Announcement
- ☐ Blog Post Follow-up
- ☐ Autoresponder Setup
- ☐ Ad Campaign
  - ○ Budget$
  - ○ Cost$
  - ○ Return$
  - ○ Click Thru Rate
  - ○ CPC (Cost per Click)
- ☐ Conversion Rate
- ☐ Hashtag
- ☐ Coupon Code (if applicable)

Campaign Sheet

Advertising Campaign

Campaign	
Boost / Ad	
Description	
Start	End
Objective	
Target Audience	
Budget$ / Cost Per Day$	
Landing Page	
Tracking Link	

Text

Demographic

Image

To Do

	Priority	Completed

Notes

Editorial Calendar

Month

SUNDAY	MONDAY	TUESDAY	WEDNESDAY	THURSDAY	FRIDAY	SATURDAY

Notes

Success Tracker

Acknowledge and Celebrate Your Success

Month:

Post with most engagement (shares, likes, and comments) on Facebook	Total Reach This Month
Most retweeted post on Twitter and number of retweets	Number of @Mentions
Most repined post on Pinterest and number of repins	Best Performing Board
Most loved Instagram photo this month and number of loves	Most Successful Hashtag
Most viewed video on YouTube and number of views	Number of videos uploaded this Month

This month I learned

A record I broke this month

My celebration this month

Next month I plan to do the same

Next month I plan to try (new)

Social Media Monthly Stats

FACEBOOK	Total Fans	New Fans	# of Posts	# of Likes	# of Comments	# of Clicks to Website
TWITTER	Total Followers	New Followers	# of Tweets	# of RT's	# of Favorites	# of Clicks to Website
GOOGLE+	Total Followers	New Followers	# of Posts	# of +1's	# of Comments	# of Clicks to Website
PINTEREST	Total Followers	New Followers	# of Pins	# of Repins	# of Likes	# of Clicks to Website
INSTAGRAM	Total Followers	New Followers	# of Pics	# of Comments/Likes		
LINKEDIN	Total Connections	New Connections	# of Posts	# of Comments/Likes		# of Clicks to Website
Other	Total Followers	New Followers	# of Posts	# of Engagement		# of Clicks to Website
EMAIL SUBSCRIBERS FROM SOCIAL MEDIA						

SOCIAL MEDIA POSTS

	Date	Posts	Post Scheduled	
Mon				
Tue				
Wed				
Thu				
Fri				
Sat				
Sun				
Mon				
Tue				
Wed				
Thu				
Fri				
Sat				
Sun				
Mon				
Tue				
Wed				
Thu				
Fri				
Sat				
Sun				
Mon				
Tue				
Wed				
Thu				
Fri				
Sat				
Sun				

Facebook

Post Ideas

- ☐ Post links, photos, events and video
- ☐ Share Blog Posts in Groups, Status Updates, and Facebook Page
- ☐ Share other's content
- ☐ Post Regularly (max 2 times a day on your page)

List Groups to Join / Start

- ☐ Add value
- ☐ Ask and respond to questions
- ☐ Post insightful comments
- ☐ Announce new members to your group

Facebook Tools

- ☐ Video – uploading video direct to Facebook gets more exposure
- ☐ Photo – create blog posts albums by category
- ☐ Apps / Tabs - Pinterest, Twitter, Instagram, email subscription etc.
- ☐ Facebook Workbook and Planner

Facebook Strategy

1. Is my preferred client using Facebook?
2. What is my objective?
3. Have I included a professional photo on my personal profile?
4. Do I have a completed Facebook Page with a logo, and branded cover?
5. About section includes keywords and URL - reflects my voice and brand.
6. Claim my custom Facebook URL.
7. Use insights to create targeted posts and know the best day and time for engagement.
8. I create super targeted ads with Facebook Advertising.
9. Integrate Facebook on my website
   - ☐ Facebook Profile buttons
   - ☐ Facebook Widget
   - ☐ Facebook Share buttons
   - ☐ Embed Facebook posts on blog posts
10. I have a (monthly/ weekly / daily) schedule for Facebook.
11. I have a (monthly/ weekly/ daily) Facebook engagement schedule.
    - ☐ Post Status Updates and in groups
    - ☐ Respond to all messages and comments on my page
    - ☐ Tag people when I post their content
    - ☐ Comment as my page
12. I have a strategy to capture leads from Facebook.
13. I have a strategy to get fans and friends to buy.
14. I always add value.
15. I am always connecting to:
    - ☐ Influencers
    - ☐ Current, Past and Future Clients
    - ☐ Future Collaborators
    - ☐ Family and Friends

Facebook Status Updates

Facebook Status Updates	Date	TIme	✓

Twitter

Post Ideas

- [ ] Post links, photos, and video
- [ ] Share Blog Posts in Groups, Status Updates and Twitter Page
- [ ] Share other's content
- [ ] Post Regularly

List Twitter Chats To Join / Start

- [ ] Add value
- [ ] Ask and respond to questions
- [ ] Post insightful comments
- [ ] Participate in niche, industry, and interests chats

Twitter Tools

- [ ] Lists – Create public and private lists
- [ ] Images and Video – Post branded photos and videos
- [ ] Twitter Cards – Add twitter cards to your website
- [ ] Twitter Workbook and Planner

Twitter Strategy

1. Is my preferred client using Twitter?
2. What is my objective?
3. Branded Bio, URL, profile image (professional photo or logo) profile header, and background image.
4. Link to other social media profiles
5. Always use #hashtags.
6. Use Twitter Analytics to create targeted posts.
7. Use Twitter Ads.
8. Integrate Twitter on my website

- [ ] Twitter Profile buttons
- [ ] Twitter Widget
- [ ] Twitter Share buttons
- [ ] Embed Twitter posts on blog posts and/or testimonials
- [ ] Use click to Tweet

9. Preface posts with comments
10. Periodically clean up my Twitter feed and unfollow spam and inactive accounts.
11. I have a (monthly/ weekly / daily) schedule for Twitter.
12. I have a (monthly/ weekly/ daily) Twitter engagement schedule.

- [ ] Update
- [ ] Retweet
- [ ] Respond
- [ ] Favorite
- [ ] Mention
- [ ] Direct Message

13. I have a strategy to capture leads from Twitter.
14. I have a strategy to get fans and friends to buy.
15. I always add value.
16. I am always connecting to:

- [ ] Influencers
- [ ] Current, Past and Future Clients
- [ ] Future Collaborators
- [ ] Family and Friends

Twitter Status Updates

Twitter Status Updates	Date	TIme	✓

LinkedIn

Post Ideas

- ☐ Utilize LinkedIn Posts
- ☐ Share Blog Posts in Groups, Status Updates, and Company Page
- ☐ Share other's content
- ☐ Links
- ☐ Post Regularly

List Groups to Join / Start

- ☐ Add value
- ☐ Ask and respond to questions
- ☐ Post insightful comments

LinkedIn Tools

- ☐ Projects – projects you have worked on and completed
- ☐ Publications – books, eBooks, workbooks, planners, etc., you have created
- ☐ Portfolio – showcase your work / creations
- ☐ LinkedIn Workbook and Planner

LinkedIn Strategy

1. Is my preferred client using LinkedIn?
2. What is my objective?
3. Have I included a professional photo?
4. Do I have a branded bio – my voice and brand?
5. Is my profile 100% complete?
6. Is my profile Search Engine Optimized?
7. My posts are compelling content and includes images
8. I have a (monthly/ weekly / daily) schedule for LinkedIn.
9. I have a (monthly/ weekly/ daily) LinkedIn engagement schedule.
   - ☐ Status Updates
   - ☐ Groups
   - ☐ Endorsements
   - ☐ Recommendations
10. I have a completed Company Page.
11. I have a strategy to capture leads from LinkedIn.
12. I have a strategy to get connections and followers to buy.
13. I always add value.
14. I am always connecting to:
    - ☐ Influencers
    - ☐ Current and Past Clients
    - ☐ Future Clients
    - ☐ Future Collaborators
    - ☐ Family and Friends

LinkedIn Status Updates

LinkedIn Status Updates	Date	TIme	✓

Google+

Post Ideas

- ☐ Post texts, links, photos, events, and video
- ☐ Share Blog Posts in Communities, Status Updates and Google+ Page
- ☐ Share other's content
- ☐ Post Regularly

List G+ Communities To Join / Start

- ☐ Add value
- ☐ Ask and respond to questions
- ☐ Post insightful comments at least once a week

Google+ Tools

- ☐ Create Targeted Circles – Influencers, clients, prospects and top engagers
- ☐ G+ Communities – Join communities and follow members
- ☐ Attend and Host G+ Hangouts – Live on air, webinar, panel discussion, video conference, video call, client meetings, screen share, etc
- ☐ Google+ Workbook and Planner

Google+ Strategy

1. Is my preferred client using Google+?
2. What is my objective?
3. Create a G+ profile page, and include professional photo.
4. Create a branded G+ Business Page (Description, Tagline, URL, logo, cover image, contact info, etc.).
5. Claim G+ authorship.
6. Claim your custom URL.
7. Share Google+ posts on other social media profiles.
8. Always use #hashtags.
9. Use keywords and descriptions.
10. Be consistent.
11. Vary posts – long and short
12. Use Google Analytics to create targeted posts.
13. Schedule posts.
14. Integrate Google+ on my website.
    - ☐ Google+ Badge
    - ☐ Google+ Profile buttons
    - ☐ Google+ Share buttons
15. I have a (monthly/ weekly / daily) schedule for Google+.
16. I have a (monthly/ weekly/ daily) Google+ engagement schedule.
    - ☐ +1
    - ☐ Comment
    - ☐ Mention (+ in front of name)
    - ☐ Respond to mentions
    - ☐ Thank people who share my content
    - ☐ Tag people when I share their content
17. I have a strategy to capture leads from Google+.
18. I always add value.
19. I am always connecting to:
    - ☐ Influencers
    - ☐ Current, Past and Future Clients
    - ☐ Future Collaborators
    - ☐ Family and Friends

Google+ Status Updates

Google+ Status Updates	Date	TIme	✓

Pinterest

Post Ideas

- ☐ Share Blog Posts on multiple boards (ensure each blog post has a pinnable image and make more than one image per blog posts)
- ☐ Share other's content
- ☐ Post Regularly

List Group Boards to Join / Start

- ☐ Add value
- ☐ Post insightful comments

Pinterest Tools

- ☐ Boards – Organize and SEO your boards with optimized board names and descriptions
- ☐ Video – Pin branded videos
- ☐ Pinterest Workbook and Planner

Pinterest Strategy

1. Is my preferred client using Pinterest?
2. What is my objective?
3. Have a I included a professional photo or logo in my profile.
4. Get verified and claim your custom Pinterest URL.
5. Use quality images.
6. Schedule posts.
7. Use #hashtags.
8. Vary vertical and horizontal images.
9. Use Pinterest Analytics to see what images people are pinning.
10. Use Pinterest Advertising.
11. Integrate Pinterest on my website
    - ☐ Pinterest Profile buttons
    - ☐ PinIt button
    - ☐ Pinterest Widget
    - ☐ Pinterest Share buttons
    - ☐ Embed Pinterest boards and posts on blog posts.
12. I have a (monthly/ weekly / daily) schedule for Pinterest.
13. I have a (monthly/ weekly/ daily) Pinterest engagement schedule.
    - ☐ Follow users
    - ☐ Like
    - ☐ Repin
    - ☐ Respond to mentions
    - ☐ Tag others
    - ☐ Comment
14. I have a strategy to capture leads from Pinterest.
15. I have a strategy to get fans and friends to buy.
16. I always add value.
17. I am always connecting to:
    - ☐ Influencers
    - ☐ Current, Past and Future Clients
    - ☐ Future Collaborators
    - ☐ Family and Friends

Pinterest Status Updates

Pins	Date	TIme	✓

Instagram

Post Ideas

- ☐ Post quality images and video
- ☐ Share Blog Posts
- ☐ Share other's content
- ☐ Post Regularly (add at least one new image daily – 2x max)

List 20 Most Used HashTags For Your Niche / Industry

- ☐ Add value
- ☐ Post insightful comments

Instagram Tools

- ☐ Filters – Visual effects over images and videos
- ☐ Video – Upload 3-15 second video directly to Instagram
- ☐ Instagram Workbook and Planner

Instagram Strategy

1. Is my preferred client using Instagram?
2. What is my objective?
3. I have a professional photo or logo on my profile.
4. I have added contact info and URL to profile
5. I have included a keyword rich bio.
6. Use short, SEO descriptions on posts.
7. Add relevant #hashtags to posts.
8. Use #hashtags in comments.
9. Use custom #hashtags on promotions, products, etc.
10. Share Instagram posts on other social media.
11. I am personable, real and authentic.
12. Integrate Instagram on my website
    - ☐ Instagram Profile buttons
    - ☐ Instagram Widget
    - ☐ Embed Instagram posts on blog posts where applicable.
13. I have a (monthly/ weekly / daily) schedule for Instagram.
14. I have a (monthly/ weekly/ daily) Instagram engagement schedule.
    - ☐ Like
    - ☐ Comment
    - ☐ Tag people
    - ☐ Follow and follow back
    - ☐ Respond to comments
15. I have a strategy to capture leads from Instagram.
16. I have a strategy to get fans and friends to buy.
17. I always add value.
18. I am always connecting to:
    - ☐ Influencers and bloggers
    - ☐ Current, Past and Future Clients
    - ☐ Future Collaborators
    - ☐ Family and Friends
    - ☐ Brands

Instagram Status Updates

Instagram Updates	Date	TIme	✓

YouTube

Post Ideas

☐ Create a video editorial calendar

☐ Reviews, demos, tutorials, testimonials and commercials

List Channels to Subscribe / Start

☐ Add value

☐ Post insightful comments

YouTube Tools

☐ Playlists – Group services, tutorials, client resources, or theme categories

☐ G+ Hangouts – Create live broadcasts on YouTube

YouTube Strategy

1. What is my YouTube marketing objective?
2. I included a professional photo on my personal profile.
3. I have a completed YouTube Channel (Icon, Art, Description, Links and URL).
4. I have created branded preview image for each video.
5. I have created a branded video intro and outro.
6. Optimize each video (Keyword in Title, Description, and Tags)
7. Use playlists.
8. Use YouTube Analytics
9. Use annotations – text, links, and graphics placed over video
10. Link to other social media platforms.
11. Integrate YouTube on my website

☐ YouTube Profile buttons

☐ YouTube Widget

☐ YouTube Share buttons

☐ Embed YouTube posts on blog posts.

12. I have a (monthly/ weekly / daily) schedule for YouTube.
13. I have a (monthly/ weekly/ daily) YouTube engagement schedule.

☐ Share videos on other social media channels.

☐ Like, share and comment on others' videos.

☐ Respond to comments.

☐ Subscribe to others' YouTube Channels.

14. I have a strategy to capture leads from YouTube.
15. I have a strategy to get fans and friends to buy.
16. I always add value.
17. I am always connecting to:

☐ Influencers

☐ Current, Past and Future Clients

☐ Future Collaborators

☐ Family and Friends

Campaign Sheet

Product / Service Campaign

Campaign	
Description	
Product / Service Newsletter Contest / Giveaway	
Start	End
Objective	
Target Audience	
Budget$ / Cost$ / Return$	
Landing Page	
Tracking Link	
Days and Time	
Winner / Date Notified	

Image

- ☐ Blog Post Announcement
- ☐ Blog Post Follow-up
- ☐ Autoresponder Setup
- ☐ Ad Campaign
  - Budget$
  - Cost$
  - Return$
  - Click Thru Rate
  - CPC (Cost per Click)
- ☐ Conversion Rate
- ☐ Hashtag
- ☐ Coupon Code (if applicable)

Campaign Sheet

Advertising Campaign

Campaign	
Boost / Ad	
Description	
Start	End
Objective	
Target Audience	
Budget$ / Cost Per Day$	
Landing Page	
Tracking Link	

Text

Demographic

Image

To Do

	Priority	Completed

Notes

Editorial Calendar

Month

SUNDAY	MONDAY	TUESDAY	WEDNESDAY	THURSDAY	FRIDAY	SATURDAY

Notes

Acknowledge and Celebrate Your Success

Month:

Post with most engagement (shares, likes, and comments) on Facebook	Total Reach This Month
Most retweeted post on Twitter and number of retweets	Number of @Mentions
Most repined post on Pinterest and number of repins	Best Performing Board
Most loved Instagram photo this month and number of loves	Most Successful Hashtag
Most viewed video on YouTube and number of views	Number of videos uploaded this Month

This month I learned

A record I broke this month

My celebration this month

Next month I plan to do the same

Next month I plan to try (new)

Social Media Monthly Stats

FACEBOOK	Total Fans	New Fans	# of Posts	# of Likes	# of Comments	# of Clicks to Website
TWITTER	Total Followers	New Followers	# of Tweets	# of RT's	# of Favorites	# of Clicks to Website
GOOGLE+	Total Followers	New Followers	# of Posts	# of +1's	# of Comments	# of Clicks to Website
PINTEREST	Total Followers	New Followers	# of Pins	# of Repins	# of Likes	# of Clicks to Website
INSTAGRAM	Total Followers	New Followers	# of Pics	# of Comments/Likes		
LINKEDIN	Total Connections	New Connections	# of Posts	# of Comments/Likes		# of Clicks to Website
Other	Total Followers	New Followers	# of Posts	# of Engagement		# of Clicks to Website
EMAIL SUBSCRIBERS FROM SOCIAL MEDIA						

Social Media Posts

	Date	Posts	Post Scheduled	
Mon				
Tue				
Wed				
Thu				
Fri				
Sat				
Sun				
Mon				
Tue				
Wed				
Thu				
Fri				
Sat				
Sun				
Mon				
Tue				
Wed				
Thu				
Fri				
Sat				
Sun				
Mon				
Tue				
Wed				
Thu				
Fri				
Sat				
Sun				

Facebook

Post Ideas

- ☐ Post links, photos, events and video
- ☐ Share Blog Posts in Groups, Status Updates, and Facebook Page
- ☐ Share other's content
- ☐ Post Regularly (max 2 times a day on your page)

List Groups to Join / Start

- ☐ Add value
- ☐ Ask and respond to questions
- ☐ Post insightful comments
- ☐ Announce new members to your group

Facebook Tools

- ☐ Video – uploading video direct to Facebook gets more exposure
- ☐ Photo – create blog posts albums by category
- ☐ Apps / Tabs - Pinterest, Twitter, Instagram, email subscription etc.
- ☐ Facebook Workbook and Planner

Facebook Strategy

1. Is my preferred client using Facebook?
2. What is my objective?
3. Have I included a professional photo on my personal profile?
4. Do I have a completed Facebook Page with a logo, and branded cover?
5. About section includes keywords and URL - reflects my voice and brand.
6. Claim my custom Facebook URL.
7. Use insights to create targeted posts and know the best day and time for engagement.
8. I create super targeted ads with Facebook Advertising.
9. Integrate Facebook on my website
   - ☐ Facebook Profile buttons
   - ☐ Facebook Widget
   - ☐ Facebook Share buttons
   - ☐ Embed Facebook posts on blog posts
10. I have a (monthly/ weekly / daily) schedule for Facebook.
11. I have a (monthly/ weekly/ daily) Facebook engagement schedule.
    - ☐ Post Status Updates and in groups
    - ☐ Respond to all messages and comments on my page
    - ☐ Tag people when I post their content
    - ☐ Comment as my page
12. I have a strategy to capture leads from Facebook.
13. I have a strategy to get fans and friends to buy.
14. I always add value.
15. I am always connecting to:
    - ☐ Influencers
    - ☐ Current, Past and Future Clients
    - ☐ Future Collaborators
    - ☐ Family and Friends

Facebook Status Updates

Facebook Status Updates	Date	TIme	✓

TWITTER

POST IDEAS

☐ Post links, photos, and video

☐ Share Blog Posts in Groups, Status Updates and Twitter Page

☐ Share other's content

☐ Post Regularly

LIST TWITTER CHATS TO JOIN / START

☐ Add value

☐ Ask and respond to questions

☐ Post insightful comments

☐ Participate in niche, industry, and interests chats

TWITTER TOOLS

☐ Lists – Create public and private lists

☐ Images and Video – Post branded photos and videos

☐ Twitter Cards – Add twitter cards to your website

☐ Twitter Workbook and Planner

TWITTER STRATEGY

1. Is my preferred client using Twitter?
2. What is my objective?
3. Branded Bio, URL, profile image (professional photo or logo) profile header, and background image.
4. Link to other social media profiles
5. Always use #hashtags.
6. Use Twitter Analytics to create targeted posts.
7. Use Twitter Ads.
8. Integrate Twitter on my website

☐ Twitter Profile buttons

☐ Twitter Widget

☐ Twitter Share buttons

☐ Embed Twitter posts on blog posts and/or testimonials

☐ Use click to Tweet

9. Preface posts with comments
10. Periodically clean up my Twitter feed and unfollow spam and inactive accounts.
11. I have a (monthly/ weekly / daily) schedule for Twitter.
12. I have a (monthly/ weekly/ daily) Twitter engagement schedule.

☐ Update ☐ Retweet

☐ Respond ☐ Favorite

☐ Mention ☐ Direct Message

13. I have a strategy to capture leads from Twitter.
14. I have a strategy to get fans and friends to buy.
15. I always add value.
16. I am always connecting to:

☐ Influencers

☐ Current, Past and Future Clients

☐ Future Collaborators

☐ Family and Friends

Twitter Status Updates

Twitter Status Updates	Date	TIme	✓

LinkedIn

Post Ideas

- ☐ Utilize LinkedIn Posts
- ☐ Share Blog Posts in Groups, Status Updates, and Company Page
- ☐ Share other's content
- ☐ Links
- ☐ Post Regularly

List Groups to Join / Start

- ☐ Add value
- ☐ Ask and respond to questions
- ☐ Post insightful comments

LinkedIn Tools

- ☐ Projects – projects you have worked on and completed
- ☐ Publications – books, eBooks, workbooks, planners, etc., you have created
- ☐ Portfolio – showcase your work / creations
- ☐ LinkedIn Workbook and Planner

LinkedIn Strategy

1. Is my preferred client using LinkedIn?
2. What is my objective?
3. Have I included a professional photo?
4. Do I have a branded bio – my voice and brand?
5. Is my profile 100% complete?
6. Is my profile Search Engine Optimized?
7. My posts are compelling content and includes images
8. I have a (monthly/ weekly / daily) schedule for LinkedIn.
9. I have a (monthly/ weekly/ daily) LinkedIn engagement schedule.
   - ☐ Status Updates
   - ☐ Groups
   - ☐ Endorsements
   - ☐ Recommendations
10. I have a completed Company Page.
11. I have a strategy to capture leads from LinkedIn.
12. I have a strategy to get connections and followers to buy.
13. I always add value.
14. I am always connecting to:
    - ☐ Influencers
    - ☐ Current and Past Clients
    - ☐ Future Clients
    - ☐ Future Collaborators
    - ☐ Family and Friends

LinkedIn Status Updates

LinkedIn Status Updates	Date	TIme	✓

Google+

Post Ideas

- ☐ Post texts, links, photos, events, and video
- ☐ Share Blog Posts in Communities, Status Updates and Google+ Page
- ☐ Share other's content
- ☐ Post Regularly

List G+ Communities To Join / Start

- ☐ Add value
- ☐ Ask and respond to questions
- ☐ Post insightful comments at least once a week

Google+ Tools

- ☐ Create Targeted Circles – Influencers, clients, prospects and top engagers
- ☐ G+ Communities – Join communities and follow members
- ☐ Attend and Host G+ Hangouts – Live on air, webinar, panel discussion, video conference, video call, client meetings, screen share, etc
- ☐ Google+ Workbook and Planner

Google+ Strategy

1. Is my preferred client using Google+?
2. What is my objective?
3. Create a G+ profile page, and include professional photo.
4. Create a branded G+ Business Page (Description, Tagline, URL, logo, cover image, contact info, etc.).
5. Claim G+ authorship.
6. Claim your custom URL.
7. Share Google+ posts on other social media profiles.
8. Always use #hashtags.
9. Use keywords and descriptions.
10. Be consistent.
11. Vary posts – long and short
12. Use Google Analytics to create targeted posts.
13. Schedule posts.
14. Integrate Google+ on my website.
    - ☐ Google+ Badge
    - ☐ Google+ Profile buttons
    - ☐ Google+ Share buttons
15. I have a (monthly/ weekly / daily) schedule for Google+.
16. I have a (monthly/ weekly/ daily) Google+ engagement schedule.
    - ☐ +1
    - ☐ Comment
    - ☐ Mention (+ in front of name)
    - ☐ Respond to mentions
    - ☐ Thank people who share my content
    - ☐ Tag people when I share their content
17. I have a strategy to capture leads from Google+.
18. I always add value.
19. I am always connecting to:
    - ☐ Influencers
    - ☐ Current, Past and Future Clients
    - ☐ Future Collaborators
    - ☐ Family and Friends

Google+ Status Updates

Google+ Status Updates	Date	TIme	✓

Pinterest

Post Ideas

☐ Share Blog Posts on multiple boards (ensure each blog post has a pinnable image and make more than one image per blog posts)

☐ Share other's content

☐ Post Regularly

List Group Boards to Join / Start

☐ Add value

☐ Post insightful comments

Pinterest Tools

☐ Boards – Organize and SEO your boards with optimized board names and descriptions

☐ Video – Pin branded videos

☐ Pinterest Workbook and Planner

Pinterest Strategy

1. Is my preferred client using Pinterest?
2. What is my objective?
3. Have a I included a professional photo or logo in my profile.
4. Get verified and claim your custom Pinterest URL.
5. Use quality images.
6. Schedule posts.
7. Use #hashtags.
8. Vary vertical and horizontal images.
9. Use Pinterest Analytics to see what images people are pinning.
10. Use Pinterest Advertising.
11. Integrate Pinterest on my website

☐ Pinterest Profile buttons

☐ PinIt button

☐ Pinterest Widget

☐ Pinterest Share buttons

☐ Embed Pinterest boards and posts on blog posts.

12. I have a (monthly/ weekly / daily) schedule for Pinterest.
13. I have a (monthly/ weekly/ daily) Pinterest engagement schedule.

☐ Follow users

☐ Like

☐ Repin

☐ Respond to mentions

☐ Tag others

☐ Comment

14. I have a strategy to capture leads from Pinterest.
15. I have a strategy to get fans and friends to buy.
16. I always add value.
17. I am always connecting to:

☐ Influencers

☐ Current, Past and Future Clients

☐ Future Collaborators

☐ Family and Friends

Pinterest Status Updates

Pins	Date	TIme	✓

Instagram

Post Ideas

- ☐ Post quality images and video
- ☐ Share Blog Posts
- ☐ Share other's content
- ☐ Post Regularly (add at least one new image daily – 2x max)

List 20 Most Used HashTags For Your Niche / Industry

- ☐ Add value
- ☐ Post insightful comments

Instagram Tools

- ☐ Filters – Visual effects over images and videos
- ☐ Video – Upload 3-15 second video directly to Instagram
- ☐ Instagram Workbook and Planner

Instagram Strategy

1. Is my preferred client using Instagram?
2. What is my objective?
3. I have a professional photo or logo on my profile.
4. I have added contact info and URL to profile
5. I have included a keyword rich bio.
6. Use short, SEO descriptions on posts.
7. Add relevant #hashtags to posts.
8. Use #hashtags in comments.
9. Use custom #hashtags on promotions, products, etc.
10. Share Instagram posts on other social media.
11. I am personable, real and authentic.
12. Integrate Instagram on my website
    - ☐ Instagram Profile buttons
    - ☐ Instagram Widget
    - ☐ Embed Instagram posts on blog posts where applicable.
13. I have a (monthly/ weekly / daily) schedule for Instagram.
14. I have a (monthly/ weekly/ daily) Instagram engagement schedule.
    - ☐ Like
    - ☐ Comment
    - ☐ Tag people
    - ☐ Follow and follow back
    - ☐ Respond to comments
15. I have a strategy to capture leads from Instagram.
16. I have a strategy to get fans and friends to buy.
17. I always add value.
18. I am always connecting to:
    - ☐ Influencers and bloggers
    - ☐ Current, Past and Future Clients
    - ☐ Future Collaborators
    - ☐ Family and Friends
    - ☐ Brands

Instagram Status Updates

Instagram Updates	Date	TIme	✓

YouTube

Post Ideas

- ☐ Create a video editorial calendar
- ☐ Reviews, demos, tutorials, testimonials and commercials

List Channels to Subscribe / Start

- ☐ Add value
- ☐ Post insightful comments

YouTube Tools

- ☐ Playlists – Group services, tutorials, client resources, or theme categories
- ☐ G+ Hangouts – Create live broadcasts on YouTube

YouTube Strategy

1. What is my YouTube marketing objective?
2. I included a professional photo on my personal profile.
3. I have a completed YouTube Channel (Icon, Art, Description, Links and URL).
4. I have created branded preview image for each video.
5. I have created a branded video intro and outro.
6. Optimize each video (Keyword in Title, Description, and Tags)
7. Use playlists.
8. Use YouTube Analytics
9. Use annotations – text, links, and graphics placed over video
10. Link to other social media platforms.
11. Integrate YouTube on my website
    - ☐ YouTube Profile buttons
    - ☐ YouTube Widget
    - ☐ YouTube Share buttons
    - ☐ Embed YouTube posts on blog posts.
12. I have a (monthly/ weekly / daily) schedule for YouTube.
13. I have a (monthly/ weekly/ daily) YouTube engagement schedule.
    - ☐ Share videos on other social media channels.
    - ☐ Like, share and comment on others' videos.
    - ☐ Respond to comments.
    - ☐ Subscribe to others' YouTube Channels.
14. I have a strategy to capture leads from YouTube.
15. I have a strategy to get fans and friends to buy.
16. I always add value.
17. I am always connecting to:
    - ☐ Influencers
    - ☐ Current, Past and Future Clients
    - ☐ Future Collaborators
    - ☐ Family and Friends

Campaign Sheet

Product / Service Campaign

Campaign	
Description	
Product / Service Newsletter Contest / Giveaway	
Start	End
Objective	
Target Audience	
Budget$ / Cost$ / Return$	
Landing Page	
Tracking Link	
Days and Time	
Winner / Date Notified	

Image

- ☐ Blog Post Announcement
- ☐ Blog Post Follow-up
- ☐ Autoresponder Setup
- ☐ Ad Campaign
  - ○ Budget$
  - ○ Cost$
  - ○ Return$
  - ○ Click Thru Rate
  - ○ CPC (Cost per Click)
- ☐ Conversion Rate
- ☐ Hashtag
- ☐ Coupon Code (if applicable)

Campaign Sheet

Advertising Campaign

Campaign	
Boost / Ad	
Description	
Start	End
Objective	
Target Audience	
Budget$ / Cost Per Day$	
Landing Page	
Tracking Link	

Text

Demographic

Image

To Do

	Priority	Completed

Notes

Editorial Calendar

Month

SUNDAY	MONDAY	TUESDAY	WEDNESDAY	THURSDAY	FRIDAY	SATURDAY

Notes

Success Tracker

Acknowledge and Celebrate Your Success

Month:

Post with most engagement (shares, likes, and comments) on Facebook	Total Reach This Month
Most retweeted post on Twitter and number of retweets	Number of @Mentions
Most repined post on Pinterest and number of repins	Best Performing Board
Most loved Instagram photo this month and number of loves	Most Successful Hashtag
Most viewed video on YouTube and number of views	Number of videos uploaded this Month

This month I learned

A record I broke this month

My celebration this month

Next month I plan to do the same

Next month I plan to try (new)

Social Media Monthly Stats

FACEBOOK	Total Fans	New Fans	# of Posts	# of Likes	# of Comments	# of Clicks to Website
TWITTER	Total Followers	New Followers	# of Tweets	# of RT's	# of Favorites	# of Clicks to Website
GOOGLE+	Total Followers	New Followers	# of Posts	# of +1's	# of Comments	# of Clicks to Website
PINTEREST	Total Followers	New Followers	# of Pins	# of Repins	# of Likes	# of Clicks to Website
INSTAGRAM	Total Followers	New Followers	# of Pics	# of Comments/Likes		
LINKEDIN	Total Connections	New Connections	# of Posts	# of Comments/Likes		# of Clicks to Website
Other	Total Followers	New Followers	# of Posts	# of Engagement		# of Clicks to Website
EMAIL SUBSCRIBERS FROM SOCIAL MEDIA						

Social Media Posts

	Date	Posts	Post Scheduled	
Mon				
Tue				
Wed				
Thu				
Fri				
Sat				
Sun				
Mon				
Tue				
Wed				
Thu				
Fri				
Sat				
Sun				
Mon				
Tue				
Wed				
Thu				
Fri				
Sat				
Sun				
Mon				
Tue				
Wed				
Thu				
Fri				
Sat				
Sun				

Facebook

Post Ideas

- ☐ Post links, photos, events and video
- ☐ Share Blog Posts in Groups, Status Updates, and Facebook Page
- ☐ Share other's content
- ☐ Post Regularly (max 2 times a day on your page)

List Groups to Join / Start

- ☐ Add value
- ☐ Ask and respond to questions
- ☐ Post insightful comments
- ☐ Announce new members to your group

Facebook Tools

- ☐ Video – uploading video direct to Facebook gets more exposure
- ☐ Photo – create blog posts albums by category
- ☐ Apps / Tabs - Pinterest, Twitter, Instagram, email subscription etc.
- ☐ Facebook Workbook and Planner

Facebook Strategy

1. Is my preferred client using Facebook?
2. What is my objective?
3. Have I included a professional photo on my personal profile?
4. Do I have a completed Facebook Page with a logo, and branded cover?
5. About section includes keywords and URL - reflects my voice and brand.
6. Claim my custom Facebook URL.
7. Use insights to create targeted posts and know the best day and time for engagement.
8. I create super targeted ads with Facebook Advertising.
9. Integrate Facebook on my website
   - ☐ Facebook Profile buttons
   - ☐ Facebook Widget
   - ☐ Facebook Share buttons
   - ☐ Embed Facebook posts on blog posts
10. I have a (monthly/ weekly / daily) schedule for Facebook.
11. I have a (monthly/ weekly/ daily) Facebook engagement schedule.
    - ☐ Post Status Updates and in groups
    - ☐ Respond to all messages and comments on my page
    - ☐ Tag people when I post their content
    - ☐ Comment as my page
12. I have a strategy to capture leads from Facebook.
13. I have a strategy to get fans and friends to buy.
14. I always add value.
15. I am always connecting to:
    - ☐ Influencers
    - ☐ Current, Past and Future Clients
    - ☐ Future Collaborators
    - ☐ Family and Friends

Facebook Status Updates

Facebook Status Updates	Date	TIme	✓

Twitter

Post Ideas

- ☐ Post links, photos, and video
- ☐ Share Blog Posts in Groups, Status Updates and Twitter Page
- ☐ Share other's content
- ☐ Post Regularly

List Twitter Chats To Join / Start

- ☐ Add value
- ☐ Ask and respond to questions
- ☐ Post insightful comments
- ☐ Participate in niche, industry, and interests chats

Twitter Tools

- ☐ Lists – Create public and private lists
- ☐ Images and Video – Post branded photos and videos
- ☐ Twitter Cards – Add twitter cards to your website
- ☐ Twitter Workbook and Planner

Twitter Strategy

1. Is my preferred client using Twitter?
2. What is my objective?
3. Branded Bio, URL, profile image (professional photo or logo) profile header, and background image.
4. Link to other social media profiles
5. Always use #hashtags.
6. Use Twitter Analytics to create targeted posts.
7. Use Twitter Ads.
8. Integrate Twitter on my website

- ☐ Twitter Profile buttons
- ☐ Twitter Widget
- ☐ Twitter Share buttons
- ☐ Embed Twitter posts on blog posts and/or testimonials
- ☐ Use click to Tweet

9. Preface posts with comments
10. Periodically clean up my Twitter feed and unfollow spam and inactive accounts.
11. I have a (monthly/ weekly / daily) schedule for Twitter.
12. I have a (monthly/ weekly/ daily) Twitter engagement schedule.

- ☐ Update
- ☐ Retweet
- ☐ Respond
- ☐ Favorite
- ☐ Mention
- ☐ Direct Message

13. I have a strategy to capture leads from Twitter.
14. I have a strategy to get fans and friends to buy.
15. I always add value.
16. I am always connecting to:

- ☐ Influencers
- ☐ Current, Past and Future Clients
- ☐ Future Collaborators
- ☐ Family and Friends

Twitter Status Updates

Twitter Status Updates	Date	TIme	✓

LinkedIn

Post Ideas

- ☐ Utilize LinkedIn Posts
- ☐ Share Blog Posts in Groups, Status Updates, and Company Page
- ☐ Share other's content
- ☐ Links
- ☐ Post Regularly

List Groups to Join / Start

- ☐ Add value
- ☐ Ask and respond to questions
- ☐ Post insightful comments

LinkedIn Tools

- ☐ Projects – projects you have worked on and completed
- ☐ Publications – books, eBooks, workbooks, planners, etc., you have created
- ☐ Portfolio – showcase your work / creations
- ☐ LinkedIn Workbook and Planner

LinkedIn Strategy

1. Is my preferred client using LinkedIn?
2. What is my objective?
3. Have I included a professional photo?
4. Do I have a branded bio – my voice and brand?
5. Is my profile 100% complete?
6. Is my profile Search Engine Optimized?
7. My posts are compelling content and includes images
8. I have a (monthly/ weekly / daily) schedule for LinkedIn.
9. I have a (monthly/ weekly/ daily) LinkedIn engagement schedule.
   - ☐ Status Updates
   - ☐ Groups
   - ☐ Endorsements
   - ☐ Recommendations
10. I have a completed Company Page.
11. I have a strategy to capture leads from LinkedIn.
12. I have a strategy to get connections and followers to buy.
13. I always add value.
14. I am always connecting to:
    - ☐ Influencers
    - ☐ Current and Past Clients
    - ☐ Future Clients
    - ☐ Future Collaborators
    - ☐ Family and Friends

LinkedIn Status Updates

LinkedIn Status Updates	Date	TIme	✓

Google+

Post Ideas

- ☐ Post texts, links, photos, events, and video
- ☐ Share Blog Posts in Communities, Status Updates and Google+ Page
- ☐ Share other's content
- ☐ Post Regularly

List G+ Communities To Join / Start

- ☐ Add value
- ☐ Ask and respond to questions
- ☐ Post insightful comments at least once a week

Google+ Tools

- ☐ Create Targeted Circles – Influencers, clients, prospects and top engagers
- ☐ G+ Communities – Join communities and follow members
- ☐ Attend and Host G+ Hangouts – Live on air, webinar, panel discussion, video conference, video call, client meetings, screen share, etc
- ☐ Google+ Workbook and Planner

Google+ Strategy

1. Is my preferred client using Google+?
2. What is my objective?
3. Create a G+ profile page, and include professional photo.
4. Create a branded G+ Business Page (Description, Tagline, URL, logo, cover image, contact info, etc.).
5. Claim G+ authorship.
6. Claim your custom URL.
7. Share Google+ posts on other social media profiles.
8. Always use #hashtags.
9. Use keywords and descriptions.
10. Be consistent.
11. Vary posts – long and short
12. Use Google Analytics to create targeted posts.
13. Schedule posts.
14. Integrate Google+ on my website.

- ☐ Google+ Badge
- ☐ Google+ Profile buttons
- ☐ Google+ Share buttons

15. I have a (monthly/ weekly / daily) schedule for Google+.
16. I have a (monthly/ weekly/ daily) Google+ engagement schedule.

- ☐ +1
- ☐ Comment
- ☐ Mention (+ in front of name)
- ☐ Respond to mentions
- ☐ Thank people who share my content
- ☐ Tag people when I share their content

17. I have a strategy to capture leads from Google+.
18. I always add value.
19. I am always connecting to:

- ☐ Influencers
- ☐ Current, Past and Future Clients
- ☐ Future Collaborators
- ☐ Family and Friends

Google+ Status Updates

Google+ Status Updates	Date	TIme	✓

Pinterest

Post Ideas

- ☐ Share Blog Posts on multiple boards (ensure each blog post has a pinnable image and make more than one image per blog posts)
- ☐ Share other's content
- ☐ Post Regularly

List Group Boards to Join / Start

- ☐ Add value
- ☐ Post insightful comments

Pinterest Tools

- ☐ Boards – Organize and SEO your boards with optimized board names and descriptions
- ☐ Video – Pin branded videos
- ☐ Pinterest Workbook and Planner

Pinterest Strategy

1. Is my preferred client using Pinterest?
2. What is my objective?
3. Have a I included a professional photo or logo in my profile.
4. Get verified and claim your custom Pinterest URL.
5. Use quality images.
6. Schedule posts.
7. Use #hashtags.
8. Vary vertical and horizontal images.
9. Use Pinterest Analytics to see what images people are pinning.
10. Use Pinterest Advertising.
11. Integrate Pinterest on my website

- ☐ Pinterest Profile buttons
- ☐ PinIt button
- ☐ Pinterest Widget
- ☐ Pinterest Share buttons
- ☐ Embed Pinterest boards and posts on blog posts.

12. I have a (monthly/ weekly / daily) schedule for Pinterest.
13. I have a (monthly/ weekly/ daily) Pinterest engagement schedule.

- ☐ Follow users
- ☐ Like
- ☐ Repin
- ☐ Respond to mentions
- ☐ Tag others
- ☐ Comment

14. I have a strategy to capture leads from Pinterest.
15. I have a strategy to get fans and friends to buy.
16. I always add value.
17. I am always connecting to:

- ☐ Influencers
- ☐ Current, Past and Future Clients
- ☐ Future Collaborators
- ☐ Family and Friends

Pinterest Status Updates

Pins	Date	TIme	✓

Instagram

Post Ideas

- ☐ Post quality images and video
- ☐ Share Blog Posts
- ☐ Share other's content
- ☐ Post Regularly (add at least one new image daily – 2x max)

List 20 Most Used HashTags For Your Niche / Industry

- ☐ Add value
- ☐ Post insightful comments

Instagram Tools

- ☐ Filters – Visual effects over images and videos
- ☐ Video – Upload 3-15 second video directly to Instagram
- ☐ Instagram Workbook and Planner

Instagram Strategy

1. Is my preferred client using Instagram?
2. What is my objective?
3. I have a professional photo or logo on my profile.
4. I have added contact info and URL to profile
5. I have included a keyword rich bio.
6. Use short, SEO descriptions on posts.
7. Add relevant #hashtags to posts.
8. Use #hashtags in comments.
9. Use custom #hashtags on promotions, products, etc.
10. Share Instagram posts on other social media.
11. I am personable, real and authentic.
12. Integrate Instagram on my website
    - ☐ Instagram Profile buttons
    - ☐ Instagram Widget
    - ☐ Embed Instagram posts on blog posts where applicable.
13. I have a (monthly/ weekly / daily) schedule for Instagram.
14. I have a (monthly/ weekly/ daily) Instagram engagement schedule.
    - ☐ Like
    - ☐ Comment
    - ☐ Tag people
    - ☐ Follow and follow back
    - ☐ Respond to comments
15. I have a strategy to capture leads from Instagram.
16. I have a strategy to get fans and friends to buy.
17. I always add value.
18. I am always connecting to:
    - ☐ Influencers and bloggers
    - ☐ Current, Past and Future Clients
    - ☐ Future Collaborators
    - ☐ Family and Friends
    - ☐ Brands

Instagram Status Updates

Instagram Updates	Date	TIme	✓

YouTube

Post Ideas

☐ Create a video editorial calendar

☐ Reviews, demos, tutorials, testimonials and commercials

List Channels to Subscribe / Start

☐ Add value

☐ Post insightful comments

YouTube Tools

☐ Playlists – Group services, tutorials, client resources, or theme categories

☐ G+ Hangouts – Create live broadcasts on YouTube

YouTube Strategy

1. What is my YouTube marketing objective?
2. I included a professional photo on my personal profile.
3. I have a completed YouTube Channel (Icon, Art, Description, Links and URL).
4. I have created branded preview image for each video.
5. I have created a branded video intro and outro.
6. Optimize each video (Keyword in Title, Description, and Tags)
7. Use playlists.
8. Use YouTube Analytics
9. Use annotations – text, links, and graphics placed over video
10. Link to other social media platforms.
11. Integrate YouTube on my website

☐ YouTube Profile buttons

☐ YouTube Widget

☐ YouTube Share buttons

☐ Embed YouTube posts on blog posts.

12. I have a (monthly/ weekly / daily) schedule for YouTube.
13. I have a (monthly/ weekly/ daily) YouTube engagement schedule.

☐ Share videos on other social media channels.

☐ Like, share and comment on others' videos.

☐ Respond to comments.

☐ Subscribe to others' YouTube Channels.

14. I have a strategy to capture leads from YouTube.
15. I have a strategy to get fans and friends to buy.
16. I always add value.
17. I am always connecting to:

☐ Influencers

☐ Current, Past and Future Clients

☐ Future Collaborators

☐ Family and Friends

Campaign Sheet

Product / Service Campaign

Campaign	
Description	
Product / Service Newsletter Contest / Giveaway	
Start	End
Objective	
Target Audience	
Budget$ / Cost$ / Return$	
Landing Page	
Tracking Link	
Days and Time	
Winner / Date Notified	

Image

- ☐ Blog Post Announcement
- ☐ Blog Post Follow-up
- ☐ Autoresponder Setup
- ☐ Ad Campaign
  - Budget$
  - Cost$
  - Return$
  - Click Thru Rate
  - CPC (Cost per Click)
- ☐ Conversion Rate
- ☐ Hashtag
- ☐ Coupon Code (if applicable)

Campaign Sheet

Advertising Campaign

Campaign	
Boost / Ad	
Description	
Start	End
Objective	
Target Audience	
Budget$ / Cost Per Day$	
Landing Page	
Tracking Link	

Text

Demographic

Image

To Do

	Priority	Completed

Notes

Editorial Calendar

Month

SUNDAY	MONDAY	TUESDAY	WEDNESDAY	THURSDAY	FRIDAY	SATURDAY

Notes

Acknowledge and Celebrate Your Success

Month:

Post with most engagement (shares, likes, and comments) on Facebook	Total Reach This Month
Most retweeted post on Twitter and number of retweets	Number of @Mentions
Most repined post on Pinterest and number of repins	Best Performing Board
Most loved Instagram photo this month and number of loves	Most Successful Hashtag
Most viewed video on YouTube and number of views	Number of videos uploaded this Month

This month I learned

A record I broke this month

My celebration this month

Next month I plan to do the same

Next month I plan to try (new)

Social Media Monthly Stats

FACEBOOK	Total Fans	New Fans	# of Posts	# of Likes	# of Comments	# of Clicks to Website
TWITTER	Total Followers	New Followers	# of Tweets	# of RT's	# of Favorites	# of Clicks to Website
GOOGLE+	Total Followers	New Followers	# of Posts	# of +1's	# of Comments	# of Clicks to Website
PINTEREST	Total Followers	New Followers	# of Pins	# of Repins	# of Likes	# of Clicks to Website
INSTAGRAM	Total Followers	New Followers	# of Pics	# of Comments/Likes		
LINKEDIN	Total Connections	New Connections	# of Posts	# of Comments/Likes		# of Clicks to Website
Other	Total Followers	New Followers	# of Posts	# of Engagement		# of Clicks to Website
EMAIL SUBSCRIBERS FROM SOCIAL MEDIA						

Social Media Posts

	Date	Posts	Post Scheduled	
Mon				
Tue				
Wed				
Thu				
Fri				
Sat				
Sun				
Mon				
Tue				
Wed				
Thu				
Fri				
Sat				
Sun				
Mon				
Tue				
Wed				
Thu				
Fri				
Sat				
Sun				
Mon				
Tue				
Wed				
Thu				
Fri				
Sat				
Sun				

Facebook

Post Ideas

- ☐ Post links, photos, events and video
- ☐ Share Blog Posts in Groups, Status Updates, and Facebook Page
- ☐ Share other's content
- ☐ Post Regularly (max 2 times a day on your page)

List Groups to Join / Start

- ☐ Add value
- ☐ Ask and respond to questions
- ☐ Post insightful comments
- ☐ Announce new members to your group

Facebook Tools

- ☐ Video – uploading video direct to Facebook gets more exposure
- ☐ Photo – create blog posts albums by category
- ☐ Apps / Tabs - Pinterest, Twitter, Instagram, email subscription etc.
- ☐ Facebook Workbook and Planner

Facebook Strategy

1. Is my preferred client using Facebook?
2. What is my objective?
3. Have I included a professional photo on my personal profile?
4. Do I have a completed Facebook Page with a logo, and branded cover?
5. About section includes keywords and URL - reflects my voice and brand.
6. Claim my custom Facebook URL.
7. Use insights to create targeted posts and know the best day and time for engagement.
8. I create super targeted ads with Facebook Advertising.
9. Integrate Facebook on my website
   - ☐ Facebook Profile buttons
   - ☐ Facebook Widget
   - ☐ Facebook Share buttons
   - ☐ Embed Facebook posts on blog posts
10. I have a (monthly/ weekly / daily) schedule for Facebook.
11. I have a (monthly/ weekly/ daily) Facebook engagement schedule.
    - ☐ Post Status Updates and in groups
    - ☐ Respond to all messages and comments on my page
    - ☐ Tag people when I post their content
    - ☐ Comment as my page
12. I have a strategy to capture leads from Facebook.
13. I have a strategy to get fans and friends to buy.
14. I always add value.
15. I am always connecting to:
    - ☐ Influencers
    - ☐ Current, Past and Future Clients
    - ☐ Future Collaborators
    - ☐ Family and Friends

Facebook Status Updates

Facebook Status Updates	Date	Time	✓

Twitter

Post Ideas

- ☐ Post links, photos, and video
- ☐ Share Blog Posts in Groups, Status Updates and Twitter Page
- ☐ Share other's content
- ☐ Post Regularly

List Twitter Chats To Join / Start

- ☐ Add value
- ☐ Ask and respond to questions
- ☐ Post insightful comments
- ☐ Participate in niche, industry, and interests chats

Twitter Tools

- ☐ Lists – Create public and private lists
- ☐ Images and Video – Post branded photos and videos
- ☐ Twitter Cards – Add twitter cards to your website
- ☐ Twitter Workbook and Planner

Twitter Strategy

1. Is my preferred client using Twitter?
2. What is my objective?
3. Branded Bio, URL, profile image (professional photo or logo) profile header, and background image.
4. Link to other social media profiles
5. Always use #hashtags.
6. Use Twitter Analytics to create targeted posts.
7. Use Twitter Ads.
8. Integrate Twitter on my website

- ☐ Twitter Profile buttons
- ☐ Twitter Widget
- ☐ Twitter Share buttons
- ☐ Embed Twitter posts on blog posts and/or testimonials
- ☐ Use click to Tweet

9. Preface posts with comments
10. Periodically clean up my Twitter feed and unfollow spam and inactive accounts.
11. I have a (monthly/ weekly / daily) schedule for Twitter.
12. I have a (monthly/ weekly/ daily) Twitter engagement schedule.

- ☐ Update
- ☐ Retweet
- ☐ Respond
- ☐ Favorite
- ☐ Mention
- ☐ Direct Message

13. I have a strategy to capture leads from Twitter.
14. I have a strategy to get fans and friends to buy.
15. I always add value.
16. I am always connecting to:

- ☐ Influencers
- ☐ Current, Past and Future Clients
- ☐ Future Collaborators
- ☐ Family and Friends

Twitter Status Updates

Twitter Status Updates	Date	TIme	✓

LinkedIn

Post Ideas

- ☐ Utilize LinkedIn Posts
- ☐ Share Blog Posts in Groups, Status Updates, and Company Page
- ☐ Share other's content
- ☐ Links
- ☐ Post Regularly

List Groups to Join / Start

- ☐ Add value
- ☐ Ask and respond to questions
- ☐ Post insightful comments

LinkedIn Tools

- ☐ Projects – projects you have worked on and completed
- ☐ Publications – books, eBooks, workbooks, planners, etc., you have created
- ☐ Portfolio – showcase your work / creations
- ☐ LinkedIn Workbook and Planner

LinkedIn Strategy

1. Is my preferred client using LinkedIn?
2. What is my objective?
3. Have I included a professional photo?
4. Do I have a branded bio – my voice and brand?
5. Is my profile 100% complete?
6. Is my profile Search Engine Optimized?
7. My posts are compelling content and includes images
8. I have a (monthly/ weekly / daily) schedule for LinkedIn.
9. I have a (monthly/ weekly/ daily) LinkedIn engagement schedule.
   - ☐ Status Updates
   - ☐ Groups
   - ☐ Endorsements
   - ☐ Recommendations
10. I have a completed Company Page.
11. I have a strategy to capture leads from LinkedIn.
12. I have a strategy to get connections and followers to buy.
13. I always add value.
14. I am always connecting to:
    - ☐ Influencers
    - ☐ Current and Past Clients
    - ☐ Future Clients
    - ☐ Future Collaborators
    - ☐ Family and Friends

LinkedIn Status Updates

LinkedIn Status Updates	Date	TIme	✓

Google+

Post Ideas

- ☐ Post texts, links, photos, events, and video
- ☐ Share Blog Posts in Communities, Status Updates and Google+ Page
- ☐ Share other's content
- ☐ Post Regularly

List G+ Communities To Join / Start

- ☐ Add value
- ☐ Ask and respond to questions
- ☐ Post insightful comments at least once a week

Google+ Tools

- ☐ Create Targeted Circles – Influencers, clients, prospects and top engagers
- ☐ G+ Communities – Join communities and follow members
- ☐ Attend and Host G+ Hangouts – Live on air, webinar, panel discussion, video conference, video call, client meetings, screen share, etc
- ☐ Google+ Workbook and Planner

Google+ Strategy

1. Is my preferred client using Google+?
2. What is my objective?
3. Create a G+ profile page, and include professional photo.
4. Create a branded G+ Business Page (Description, Tagline, URL, logo, cover image, contact info, etc.).
5. Claim G+ authorship.
6. Claim your custom URL.
7. Share Google+ posts on other social media profiles.
8. Always use #hashtags.
9. Use keywords and descriptions.
10. Be consistent.
11. Vary posts – long and short
12. Use Google Analytics to create targeted posts.
13. Schedule posts.
14. Integrate Google+ on my website.
    - ☐ Google+ Badge
    - ☐ Google+ Profile buttons
    - ☐ Google+ Share buttons
15. I have a (monthly/ weekly / daily) schedule for Google+.
16. I have a (monthly/ weekly/ daily) Google+ engagement schedule.
    - ☐ +1
    - ☐ Comment
    - ☐ Mention (+ in front of name)
    - ☐ Respond to mentions
    - ☐ Thank people who share my content
    - ☐ Tag people when I share their content
17. I have a strategy to capture leads from Google+.
18. I always add value.
19. I am always connecting to:
    - ☐ Influencers
    - ☐ Current, Past and Future Clients
    - ☐ Future Collaborators
    - ☐ Family and Friends

Google+ Status Updates

Google+ Status Updates	Date	TIme	✓

Pinterest

Post Ideas

☐ Share Blog Posts on multiple boards (ensure each blog post has a pinnable image and make more than one image per blog posts)

☐ Share other's content

☐ Post Regularly

List Group Boards to Join / Start

☐ Add value

☐ Post insightful comments

Pinterest Tools

☐ Boards – Organize and SEO your boards with optimized board names and descriptions

☐ Video – Pin branded videos

☐ Pinterest Workbook and Planner

Pinterest Strategy

1. Is my preferred client using Pinterest?
2. What is my objective?
3. Have a I included a professional photo or logo in my profile.
4. Get verified and claim your custom Pinterest URL.
5. Use quality images.
6. Schedule posts.
7. Use #hashtags.
8. Vary vertical and horizontal images.
9. Use Pinterest Analytics to see what images people are pinning.
10. Use Pinterest Advertising.
11. Integrate Pinterest on my website

☐ Pinterest Profile buttons

☐ PinIt button

☐ Pinterest Widget

☐ Pinterest Share buttons

☐ Embed Pinterest boards and posts on blog posts.

12. I have a (monthly/ weekly / daily) schedule for Pinterest.
13. I have a (monthly/ weekly/ daily) Pinterest engagement schedule.

☐ Follow users

☐ Like

☐ Repin

☐ Respond to mentions

☐ Tag others

☐ Comment

14. I have a strategy to capture leads from Pinterest.
15. I have a strategy to get fans and friends to buy.
16. I always add value.
17. I am always connecting to:

☐ Influencers

☐ Current, Past and Future Clients

☐ Future Collaborators

☐ Family and Friends

Pinterest Status Updates

Pins	Date	TIme	✓

Instagram

Post Ideas

- ☐ Post quality images and video
- ☐ Share Blog Posts
- ☐ Share other's content
- ☐ Post Regularly (add at least one new image daily – 2x max)

List 20 Most Used HashTags For Your Niche / Industry

- ☐ Add value
- ☐ Post insightful comments

Instagram Tools

- ☐ Filters – Visual effects over images and videos
- ☐ Video – Upload 3-15 second video directly to Instagram
- ☐ Instagram Workbook and Planner

Instagram Strategy

1. Is my preferred client using Instagram?
2. What is my objective?
3. I have a professional photo or logo on my profile.
4. I have added contact info and URL to profile
5. I have included a keyword rich bio.
6. Use short, SEO descriptions on posts.
7. Add relevant #hashtags to posts.
8. Use #hashtags in comments.
9. Use custom #hashtags on promotions, products, etc.
10. Share Instagram posts on other social media.
11. I am personable, real and authentic.
12. Integrate Instagram on my website
    - ☐ Instagram Profile buttons
    - ☐ Instagram Widget
    - ☐ Embed Instagram posts on blog posts where applicable.
13. I have a (monthly/ weekly / daily) schedule for Instagram.
14. I have a (monthly/ weekly/ daily) Instagram engagement schedule.
    - ☐ Like
    - ☐ Comment
    - ☐ Tag people
    - ☐ Follow and follow back
    - ☐ Respond to comments
15. I have a strategy to capture leads from Instagram.
16. I have a strategy to get fans and friends to buy.
17. I always add value.
18. I am always connecting to:
    - ☐ Influencers and bloggers
    - ☐ Current, Past and Future Clients
    - ☐ Future Collaborators
    - ☐ Family and Friends
    - ☐ Brands

Instagram Status Updates

Instagram Updates	Date	TIme	✓

YouTube

Post Ideas

- ☐ Create a video editorial calendar
- ☐ Reviews, demos, tutorials, testimonials and commercials

List Channels to Subscribe / Start

- ☐ Add value
- ☐ Post insightful comments

YouTube Tools

- ☐ Playlists – Group services, tutorials, client resources, or theme categories
- ☐ G+ Hangouts – Create live broadcasts on YouTube

YouTube Strategy

1. What is my YouTube marketing objective?
2. I included a professional photo on my personal profile.
3. I have a completed YouTube Channel (Icon, Art, Description, Links and URL).
4. I have created branded preview image for each video.
5. I have created a branded video intro and outro.
6. Optimize each video (Keyword in Title, Description, and Tags)
7. Use playlists.
8. Use YouTube Analytics
9. Use annotations – text, links, and graphics placed over video
10. Link to other social media platforms.
11. Integrate YouTube on my website

- ☐ YouTube Profile buttons
- ☐ YouTube Widget
- ☐ YouTube Share buttons
- ☐ Embed YouTube posts on blog posts.

12. I have a (monthly/ weekly / daily) schedule for YouTube.
13. I have a (monthly/ weekly/ daily) YouTube engagement schedule.

- ☐ Share videos on other social media channels.
- ☐ Like, share and comment on others' videos.
- ☐ Respond to comments.
- ☐ Subscribe to others' YouTube Channels.

14. I have a strategy to capture leads from YouTube.
15. I have a strategy to get fans and friends to buy.
16. I always add value.
17. I am always connecting to:

- ☐ Influencers
- ☐ Current, Past and Future Clients
- ☐ Future Collaborators
- ☐ Family and Friends

Campaign Sheet

Product / Service Campaign

Campaign	
Description	
Product / Service Newsletter Contest / Giveaway	
Start	End
Objective	
Target Audience	
Budget$ / Cost$ / Return$	
Landing Page	
Tracking Link	
Days and Time	
Winner / Date Notified	

Image

- ☐ Blog Post Announcement
- ☐ Blog Post Follow-up
- ☐ Autoresponder Setup
- ☐ Ad Campaign
  - Budget$
  - Cost$
  - Return$
  - Click Thru Rate
  - CPC (Cost per Click)
- ☐ Conversion Rate
- ☐ Hashtag
- ☐ Coupon Code (if applicable)

Campaign Sheet

Advertising Campaign

Campaign	
Boost / Ad	
Description	
Start	End
Objective	
Target Audience	
Budget$ / Cost Per Day$	
Landing Page	
Tracking Link	

Text

Demographic

Image

To Do

	Priority	Completed

Notes

Editorial Calendar

Month

SUNDAY	MONDAY	TUESDAY	WEDNESDAY	THURSDAY	FRIDAY	SATURDAY

Notes

Acknowledge and Celebrate Your Success

Month:

Post with most engagement (shares, likes, and comments) on Facebook	Total Reach This Month
Most retweeted post on Twitter and number of retweets	Number of @Mentions
Most repined post on Pinterest and number of repins	Best Performing Board
Most loved Instagram photo this month and number of loves	Most Successful Hashtag
Most viewed video on YouTube and number of views	Number of videos uploaded this Month

This month I learned

A record I broke this month

My celebration this month

Next month I plan to do the same

Next month I plan to try (new)

Social Media Monthly Stats

FACEBOOK	Total Fans	New Fans	# of Posts	# of Likes	# of Comments	# of Clicks to Website
TWITTER	Total Followers	New Followers	# of Tweets	# of RT's	# of Favorites	# of Clicks to Website
GOOGLE+	Total Followers	New Followers	# of Posts	# of +1's	# of Comments	# of Clicks to Website
PINTEREST	Total Followers	New Followers	# of Pins	# of Repins	# of Likes	# of Clicks to Website
INSTAGRAM	Total Followers	New Followers	# of Pics	# of Comments/Likes		
LINKEDIN	Total Connections	New Connections	# of Posts	# of Comments/Likes		# of Clicks to Website
Other	Total Followers	New Followers	# of Posts	# of Engagement		# of Clicks to Website
EMAIL SUBSCRIBERS FROM SOCIAL MEDIA						

Social Media Posts

	Date	Posts	Post Scheduled	
Mon				
Tue				
Wed				
Thu				
Fri				
Sat				
Sun				
Mon				
Tue				
Wed				
Thu				
Fri				
Sat				
Sun				
Mon				
Tue				
Wed				
Thu				
Fri				
Sat				
Sun				
Mon				
Tue				
Wed				
Thu				
Fri				
Sat				
Sun				

Facebook

Post Ideas

- ☐ Post links, photos, events and video
- ☐ Share Blog Posts in Groups, Status Updates, and Facebook Page
- ☐ Share other's content
- ☐ Post Regularly (max 2 times a day on your page)

List Groups to Join / Start

- ☐ Add value
- ☐ Ask and respond to questions
- ☐ Post insightful comments
- ☐ Announce new members to your group

Facebook Tools

- ☐ Video – uploading video direct to Facebook gets more exposure
- ☐ Photo – create blog posts albums by category
- ☐ Apps / Tabs - Pinterest, Twitter, Instagram, email subscription etc.
- ☐ Facebook Workbook and Planner

Facebook Strategy

1. Is my preferred client using Facebook?
2. What is my objective?
3. Have I included a professional photo on my personal profile?
4. Do I have a completed Facebook Page with a logo, and branded cover?
5. About section includes keywords and URL - reflects my voice and brand.
6. Claim my custom Facebook URL.
7. Use insights to create targeted posts and know the best day and time for engagement.
8. I create super targeted ads with Facebook Advertising.
9. Integrate Facebook on my website
   - ☐ Facebook Profile buttons
   - ☐ Facebook Widget
   - ☐ Facebook Share buttons
   - ☐ Embed Facebook posts on blog posts
10. I have a (monthly/ weekly / daily) schedule for Facebook.
11. I have a (monthly/ weekly/ daily) Facebook engagement schedule.
    - ☐ Post Status Updates and in groups
    - ☐ Respond to all messages and comments on my page
    - ☐ Tag people when I post their content
    - ☐ Comment as my page
12. I have a strategy to capture leads from Facebook.
13. I have a strategy to get fans and friends to buy.
14. I always add value.
15. I am always connecting to:
    - ☐ Influencers
    - ☐ Current, Past and Future Clients
    - ☐ Future Collaborators
    - ☐ Family and Friends

Facebook Status Updates

Facebook Status Updates	Date	TIme	✓

Twitter

Post Ideas

- ☐ Post links, photos, and video
- ☐ Share Blog Posts in Groups, Status Updates and Twitter Page
- ☐ Share other's content
- ☐ Post Regularly

List Twitter Chats To Join / Start

- ☐ Add value
- ☐ Ask and respond to questions
- ☐ Post insightful comments
- ☐ Participate in niche, industry, and interests chats

Twitter Tools

- ☐ Lists – Create public and private lists
- ☐ Images and Video – Post branded photos and videos
- ☐ Twitter Cards – Add twitter cards to your website
- ☐ Twitter Workbook and Planner

Twitter Strategy

1. Is my preferred client using Twitter?
2. What is my objective?
3. Branded Bio, URL, profile image (professional photo or logo) profile header, and background image.
4. Link to other social media profiles
5. Always use #hashtags.
6. Use Twitter Analytics to create targeted posts.
7. Use Twitter Ads.
8. Integrate Twitter on my website

- ☐ Twitter Profile buttons
- ☐ Twitter Widget
- ☐ Twitter Share buttons
- ☐ Embed Twitter posts on blog posts and/or testimonials
- ☐ Use click to Tweet

9. Preface posts with comments
10. Periodically clean up my Twitter feed and unfollow spam and inactive accounts.
11. I have a (monthly/ weekly / daily) schedule for Twitter.
12. I have a (monthly/ weekly/ daily) Twitter engagement schedule.

- ☐ Update
- ☐ Retweet
- ☐ Respond
- ☐ Favorite
- ☐ Mention
- ☐ Direct Message

13. I have a strategy to capture leads from Twitter.
14. I have a strategy to get fans and friends to buy.
15. I always add value.
16. I am always connecting to:

- ☐ Influencers
- ☐ Current, Past and Future Clients
- ☐ Future Collaborators
- ☐ Family and Friends

Twitter Status Updates

Twitter Status Updates	Date	TIme	✓

LinkedIn

Post Ideas

- ☐ Utilize LinkedIn Posts
- ☐ Share Blog Posts in Groups, Status Updates, and Company Page
- ☐ Share other's content
- ☐ Links
- ☐ Post Regularly

List Groups to Join / Start

- ☐ Add value
- ☐ Ask and respond to questions
- ☐ Post insightful comments

LinkedIn Tools

- ☐ Projects – projects you have worked on and completed
- ☐ Publications – books, eBooks, workbooks, planners, etc., you have created
- ☐ Portfolio – showcase your work / creations
- ☐ LinkedIn Workbook and Planner

LinkedIn Strategy

1. Is my preferred client using LinkedIn?
2. What is my objective?
3. Have I included a professional photo?
4. Do I have a branded bio – my voice and brand?
5. Is my profile 100% complete?
6. Is my profile Search Engine Optimized?
7. My posts are compelling content and includes images
8. I have a (monthly/ weekly / daily) schedule for LinkedIn.
9. I have a (monthly/ weekly/ daily) LinkedIn engagement schedule.
   - ☐ Status Updates
   - ☐ Groups
   - ☐ Endorsements
   - ☐ Recommendations
10. I have a completed Company Page.
11. I have a strategy to capture leads from LinkedIn.
12. I have a strategy to get connections and followers to buy.
13. I always add value.
14. I am always connecting to:
    - ☐ Influencers
    - ☐ Current and Past Clients
    - ☐ Future Clients
    - ☐ Future Collaborators
    - ☐ Family and Friends

LinkedIn Status Updates

LinkedIn Status Updates	Date	TIme	✓

Google+

Post Ideas

- ☐ Post texts, links, photos, events, and video
- ☐ Share Blog Posts in Communities, Status Updates and Google+ Page
- ☐ Share other's content
- ☐ Post Regularly

List G+ Communities To Join / Start

- ☐ Add value
- ☐ Ask and respond to questions
- ☐ Post insightful comments at least once a week

Google+ Tools

- ☐ Create Targeted Circles – Influencers, clients, prospects and top engagers
- ☐ G+ Communities – Join communities and follow members
- ☐ Attend and Host G+ Hangouts – Live on air, webinar, panel discussion, video conference, video call, client meetings, screen share, etc
- ☐ Google+ Workbook and Planner

Google+ Strategy

1. Is my preferred client using Google+?
2. What is my objective?
3. Create a G+ profile page, and include professional photo.
4. Create a branded G+ Business Page (Description, Tagline, URL, logo, cover image, contact info, etc.).
5. Claim G+ authorship.
6. Claim your custom URL.
7. Share Google+ posts on other social media profiles.
8. Always use #hashtags.
9. Use keywords and descriptions.
10. Be consistent.
11. Vary posts – long and short
12. Use Google Analytics to create targeted posts.
13. Schedule posts.
14. Integrate Google+ on my website.

- ☐ Google+ Badge
- ☐ Google+ Profile buttons
- ☐ Google+ Share buttons

15. I have a (monthly/ weekly / daily) schedule for Google+.
16. I have a (monthly/ weekly/ daily) Google+ engagement schedule.

- ☐ +1
- ☐ Comment
- ☐ Mention (+ in front of name)
- ☐ Respond to mentions
- ☐ Thank people who share my content
- ☐ Tag people when I share their content

17. I have a strategy to capture leads from Google+.
18. I always add value.
19. I am always connecting to:

- ☐ Influencers
- ☐ Current, Past and Future Clients
- ☐ Future Collaborators
- ☐ Family and Friends

Google+ Status Updates

Google+ Status Updates	Date	TIme	✓

Pinterest

Post Ideas

- ☐ Share Blog Posts on multiple boards (ensure each blog post has a pinnable image and make more than one image per blog posts)
- ☐ Share other's content
- ☐ Post Regularly

List Group Boards to Join / Start

- ☐ Add value
- ☐ Post insightful comments

Pinterest Tools

- ☐ Boards – Organize and SEO your boards with optimized board names and descriptions
- ☐ Video – Pin branded videos
- ☐ Pinterest Workbook and Planner

Pinterest Strategy

1. Is my preferred client using Pinterest?
2. What is my objective?
3. Have a I included a professional photo or logo in my profile.
4. Get verified and claim your custom Pinterest URL.
5. Use quality images.
6. Schedule posts.
7. Use #hashtags.
8. Vary vertical and horizontal images.
9. Use Pinterest Analytics to see what images people are pinning.
10. Use Pinterest Advertising.
11. Integrate Pinterest on my website
    - ☐ Pinterest Profile buttons
    - ☐ PinIt button
    - ☐ Pinterest Widget
    - ☐ Pinterest Share buttons
    - ☐ Embed Pinterest boards and posts on blog posts.
12. I have a (monthly/ weekly / daily) schedule for Pinterest.
13. I have a (monthly/ weekly/ daily) Pinterest engagement schedule.
    - ☐ Follow users
    - ☐ Like
    - ☐ Repin
    - ☐ Respond to mentions
    - ☐ Tag others
    - ☐ Comment
14. I have a strategy to capture leads from Pinterest.
15. I have a strategy to get fans and friends to buy.
16. I always add value.
17. I am always connecting to:
    - ☐ Influencers
    - ☐ Current, Past and Future Clients
    - ☐ Future Collaborators
    - ☐ Family and Friends

Pinterest Status Updates

Pins	Date	TIme	✓

Instagram

Post Ideas

☐ Post quality images and video

☐ Share Blog Posts

☐ Share other's content

☐ Post Regularly (add at least one new image daily – 2x max)

List 20 Most Used HashTags For Your Niche / Industry

☐ Add value

☐ Post insightful comments

Instagram Tools

☐ Filters – Visual effects over images and videos

☐ Video – Upload 3-15 second video directly to Instagram

☐ Instagram Workbook and Planner

Instagram Strategy

1. Is my preferred client using Instagram?
2. What is my objective?
3. I have a professional photo or logo on my profile.
4. I have added contact info and URL to profile
5. I have included a keyword rich bio.
6. Use short, SEO descriptions on posts.
7. Add relevant #hashtags to posts.
8. Use #hashtags in comments.
9. Use custom #hashtags on promotions, products, etc.
10. Share Instagram posts on other social media.
11. I am personable, real and authentic.
12. Integrate Instagram on my website

☐ Instagram Profile buttons

☐ Instagram Widget

☐ Embed Instagram posts on blog posts where applicable.

13. I have a (monthly/ weekly / daily) schedule for Instagram.
14. I have a (monthly/ weekly/ daily) Instagram engagement schedule.

☐ Like

☐ Comment

☐ Tag people

☐ Follow and follow back

☐ Respond to comments

15. I have a strategy to capture leads from Instagram.
16. I have a strategy to get fans and friends to buy.
17. I always add value.
18. I am always connecting to:

☐ Influencers and bloggers

☐ Current, Past and Future Clients

☐ Future Collaborators

☐ Family and Friends

☐ Brands

Instagram Status Updates

Instagram Updates	Date	TIme	✓

YouTube

Post Ideas

☐ Create a video editorial calendar

☐ Reviews, demos, tutorials, testimonials and commercials

List Channels to Subscribe / Start

☐ Add value

☐ Post insightful comments

YouTube Tools

☐ Playlists – Group services, tutorials, client resources, or theme categories

☐ G+ Hangouts – Create live broadcasts on YouTube

YouTube Strategy

1. What is my YouTube marketing objective?
2. I included a professional photo on my personal profile.
3. I have a completed YouTube Channel (Icon, Art, Description, Links and URL).
4. I have created branded preview image for each video.
5. I have created a branded video intro and outro.
6. Optimize each video (Keyword in Title, Description, and Tags)
7. Use playlists.
8. Use YouTube Analytics
9. Use annotations – text, links, and graphics placed over video
10. Link to other social media platforms.
11. Integrate YouTube on my website

☐ YouTube Profile buttons

☐ YouTube Widget

☐ YouTube Share buttons

☐ Embed YouTube posts on blog posts.

12. I have a (monthly/ weekly / daily) schedule for YouTube.
13. I have a (monthly/ weekly/ daily) YouTube engagement schedule.

☐ Share videos on other social media channels.

☐ Like, share and comment on others' videos.

☐ Respond to comments.

☐ Subscribe to others' YouTube Channels.

14. I have a strategy to capture leads from YouTube.
15. I have a strategy to get fans and friends to buy.
16. I always add value.
17. I am always connecting to:

☐ Influencers

☐ Current, Past and Future Clients

☐ Future Collaborators

☐ Family and Friends

Campaign Sheet

Product / Service Campaign

Campaign	
Description	
Product / Service Newsletter Contest / Giveaway	
Start	End
Objective	
Target Audience	
Budget$ / Cost$ / Return$	
Landing Page	
Tracking Link	
Days and Time	
Winner / Date Notified	

Image

- ☐ Blog Post Announcement
- ☐ Blog Post Follow-up
- ☐ Autoresponder Setup
- ☐ Ad Campaign
  - Budget$
  - Cost$
  - Return$
  - Click Thru Rate
  - CPC (Cost per Click)
- ☐ Conversion Rate
- ☐ Hashtag
- ☐ Coupon Code (if applicable)

Campaign Sheet

Advertising Campaign

Campaign	
Boost / Ad	
Description	
Start	End
Objective	
Target Audience	
Budget$ / Cost Per Day$	
Landing Page	
Tracking Link	

Text

Demographic

Image

To Do

	Priority	Completed

Notes

Editorial Calendar

Month

SUNDAY	MONDAY	TUESDAY	WEDNESDAY	THURSDAY	FRIDAY	SATURDAY

Notes

Acknowledge and Celebrate Your Success

Month:

Post with most engagement (shares, likes, and comments) on Facebook	Total Reach This Month
Most retweeted post on Twitter and number of retweets	Number of @Mentions
Most repined post on Pinterest and number of repins	Best Performing Board
Most loved Instagram photo this month and number of loves	Most Successful Hashtag
Most viewed video on YouTube and number of views	Number of videos uploaded this Month

This month I learned

A record I broke this month

My celebration this month

Next month I plan to do the same

Next month I plan to try (new)

Social Media Monthly Stats

FACEBOOK	Total Fans	New Fans	# of Posts	# of Likes	# of Comments	# of Clicks to Website
TWITTER	Total Followers	New Followers	# of Tweets	# of RT's	# of Favorites	# of Clicks to Website
GOOGLE+	Total Followers	New Followers	# of Posts	# of +1's	# of Comments	# of Clicks to Website
PINTEREST	Total Followers	New Followers	# of Pins	# of Repins	# of Likes	# of Clicks to Website
INSTAGRAM	Total Followers	New Followers	# of Pics	# of Comments/Likes		
LINKEDIN	Total Connections	New Connections	# of Posts	# of Comments/Likes		# of Clicks to Website
Other	Total Followers	New Followers	# of Posts	# of Engagement		# of Clicks to Website
EMAIL SUBSCRIBERS FROM SOCIAL MEDIA						

Social Media Posts

	Date	Posts	Post Scheduled	
Mon				
Tue				
Wed				
Thu				
Fri				
Sat				
Sun				
Mon				
Tue				
Wed				
Thu				
Fri				
Sat				
Sun				
Mon				
Tue				
Wed				
Thu				
Fri				
Sat				
Sun				
Mon				
Tue				
Wed				
Thu				
Fri				
Sat				
Sun				

Facebook

Post Ideas

- ☐ Post links, photos, events and video
- ☐ Share Blog Posts in Groups, Status Updates, and Facebook Page
- ☐ Share other's content
- ☐ Post Regularly (max 2 times a day on your page)

List Groups to Join / Start

- ☐ Add value
- ☐ Ask and respond to questions
- ☐ Post insightful comments
- ☐ Announce new members to your group

Facebook Tools

- ☐ Video – uploading video direct to Facebook gets more exposure
- ☐ Photo – create blog posts albums by category
- ☐ Apps / Tabs - Pinterest, Twitter, Instagram, email subscription etc.
- ☐ Facebook Workbook and Planner

Facebook Strategy

1. Is my preferred client using Facebook?
2. What is my objective?
3. Have I included a professional photo on my personal profile?
4. Do I have a completed Facebook Page with a logo, and branded cover?
5. About section includes keywords and URL - reflects my voice and brand.
6. Claim my custom Facebook URL.
7. Use insights to create targeted posts and know the best day and time for engagement.
8. I create super targeted ads with Facebook Advertising.
9. Integrate Facebook on my website

- ☐ Facebook Profile buttons
- ☐ Facebook Widget
- ☐ Facebook Share buttons
- ☐ Embed Facebook posts on blog posts

10. I have a (monthly/ weekly / daily) schedule for Facebook.
11. I have a (monthly/ weekly/ daily) Facebook engagement schedule.

- ☐ Post Status Updates and in groups
- ☐ Respond to all messages and comments on my page
- ☐ Tag people when I post their content
- ☐ Comment as my page

12. I have a strategy to capture leads from Facebook.
13. I have a strategy to get fans and friends to buy.
14. I always add value.
15. I am always connecting to:

- ☐ Influencers
- ☐ Current, Past and Future Clients
- ☐ Future Collaborators
- ☐ Family and Friends

Facebook Status Updates

Facebook Status Updates	Date	TIme	✓

Twitter

Post Ideas

- ☐ Post links, photos, and video
- ☐ Share Blog Posts in Groups, Status Updates and Twitter Page
- ☐ Share other's content
- ☐ Post Regularly

List Twitter Chats To Join / Start

- ☐ Add value
- ☐ Ask and respond to questions
- ☐ Post insightful comments
- ☐ Participate in niche, industry, and interests chats

Twitter Tools

- ☐ Lists – Create public and private lists
- ☐ Images and Video – Post branded photos and videos
- ☐ Twitter Cards – Add twitter cards to your website
- ☐ Twitter Workbook and Planner

Twitter Strategy

1. Is my preferred client using Twitter?
2. What is my objective?
3. Branded Bio, URL, profile image (professional photo or logo) profile header, and background image.
4. Link to other social media profiles
5. Always use #hashtags.
6. Use Twitter Analytics to create targeted posts.
7. Use Twitter Ads.
8. Integrate Twitter on my website

- ☐ Twitter Profile buttons
- ☐ Twitter Widget
- ☐ Twitter Share buttons
- ☐ Embed Twitter posts on blog posts and/or testimonials
- ☐ Use click to Tweet

9. Preface posts with comments
10. Periodically clean up my Twitter feed and unfollow spam and inactive accounts.
11. I have a (monthly/ weekly / daily) schedule for Twitter.
12. I have a (monthly/ weekly/ daily) Twitter engagement schedule.

- ☐ Update
- ☐ Retweet
- ☐ Respond
- ☐ Favorite
- ☐ Mention
- ☐ Direct Message

13. I have a strategy to capture leads from Twitter.
14. I have a strategy to get fans and friends to buy.
15. I always add value.
16. I am always connecting to:

- ☐ Influencers
- ☐ Current, Past and Future Clients
- ☐ Future Collaborators
- ☐ Family and Friends

Twitter Status Updates

Twitter Status Updates	Date	TIme	✓

LinkedIn

Post Ideas

- ☐ Utilize LinkedIn Posts
- ☐ Share Blog Posts in Groups, Status Updates, and Company Page
- ☐ Share other's content
- ☐ Links
- ☐ Post Regularly

List Groups to Join / Start

- ☐ Add value
- ☐ Ask and respond to questions
- ☐ Post insightful comments

LinkedIn Tools

- ☐ Projects – projects you have worked on and completed
- ☐ Publications – books, eBooks, workbooks, planners, etc., you have created
- ☐ Portfolio – showcase your work / creations
- ☐ LinkedIn Workbook and Planner

LinkedIn Strategy

1. Is my preferred client using LinkedIn?
2. What is my objective?
3. Have I included a professional photo?
4. Do I have a branded bio – my voice and brand?
5. Is my profile 100% complete?
6. Is my profile Search Engine Optimized?
7. My posts are compelling content and includes images
8. I have a (monthly/ weekly / daily) schedule for LinkedIn.
9. I have a (monthly/ weekly/ daily) LinkedIn engagement schedule.
   - ☐ Status Updates
   - ☐ Groups
   - ☐ Endorsements
   - ☐ Recommendations
10. I have a completed Company Page.
11. I have a strategy to capture leads from LinkedIn.
12. I have a strategy to get connections and followers to buy.
13. I always add value.
14. I am always connecting to:
    - ☐ Influencers
    - ☐ Current and Past Clients
    - ☐ Future Clients
    - ☐ Future Collaborators
    - ☐ Family and Friends

LinkedIn Status Updates

LinkedIn Status Updates	Date	TIme	✓

Google+

Post Ideas

- ☐ Post texts, links, photos, events, and video
- ☐ Share Blog Posts in Communities, Status Updates and Google+ Page
- ☐ Share other's content
- ☐ Post Regularly

List G+ Communities To Join / Start

- ☐ Add value
- ☐ Ask and respond to questions
- ☐ Post insightful comments at least once a week

Google+ Tools

- ☐ Create Targeted Circles – Influencers, clients, prospects and top engagers
- ☐ G+ Communities – Join communities and follow members
- ☐ Attend and Host G+ Hangouts – Live on air, webinar, panel discussion, video conference, video call, client meetings, screen share, etc
- ☐ Google+ Workbook and Planner

Google+ Strategy

1. Is my preferred client using Google+?
2. What is my objective?
3. Create a G+ profile page, and include professional photo.
4. Create a branded G+ Business Page (Description, Tagline, URL, logo, cover image, contact info, etc.).
5. Claim G+ authorship.
6. Claim your custom URL.
7. Share Google+ posts on other social media profiles.
8. Always use #hashtags.
9. Use keywords and descriptions.
10. Be consistent.
11. Vary posts – long and short
12. Use Google Analytics to create targeted posts.
13. Schedule posts.
14. Integrate Google+ on my website.
    - ☐ Google+ Badge
    - ☐ Google+ Profile buttons
    - ☐ Google+ Share buttons
15. I have a (monthly/ weekly / daily) schedule for Google+.
16. I have a (monthly/ weekly/ daily) Google+ engagement schedule.
    - ☐ +1
    - ☐ Comment
    - ☐ Mention (+ in front of name)
    - ☐ Respond to mentions
    - ☐ Thank people who share my content
    - ☐ Tag people when I share their content
17. I have a strategy to capture leads from Google+.
18. I always add value.
19. I am always connecting to:
    - ☐ Influencers
    - ☐ Current, Past and Future Clients
    - ☐ Future Collaborators
    - ☐ Family and Friends

Google+ Status Updates

Google+ Status Updates	Date	TIme	✓

Pinterest

Post Ideas

- ☐ Share Blog Posts on multiple boards (ensure each blog post has a pinnable image and make more than one image per blog posts)
- ☐ Share other's content
- ☐ Post Regularly

List Group Boards to Join / Start

- ☐ Add value
- ☐ Post insightful comments

Pinterest Tools

- ☐ Boards – Organize and SEO your boards with optimized board names and descriptions
- ☐ Video – Pin branded videos
- ☐ Pinterest Workbook and Planner

Pinterest Strategy

1. Is my preferred client using Pinterest?
2. What is my objective?
3. Have a I included a professional photo or logo in my profile.
4. Get verified and claim your custom Pinterest URL.
5. Use quality images.
6. Schedule posts.
7. Use #hashtags.
8. Vary vertical and horizontal images.
9. Use Pinterest Analytics to see what images people are pinning.
10. Use Pinterest Advertising.
11. Integrate Pinterest on my website

- ☐ Pinterest Profile buttons
- ☐ PinIt button
- ☐ Pinterest Widget
- ☐ Pinterest Share buttons
- ☐ Embed Pinterest boards and posts on blog posts.

12. I have a (monthly/ weekly / daily) schedule for Pinterest.
13. I have a (monthly/ weekly/ daily) Pinterest engagement schedule.

- ☐ Follow users
- ☐ Like
- ☐ Repin
- ☐ Respond to mentions
- ☐ Tag others
- ☐ Comment

14. I have a strategy to capture leads from Pinterest.
15. I have a strategy to get fans and friends to buy.
16. I always add value.
17. I am always connecting to:

- ☐ Influencers
- ☐ Current, Past and Future Clients
- ☐ Future Collaborators
- ☐ Family and Friends

Pinterest Status Updates

Pins	Date	TIme	✓

Instagram

Post Ideas

- ☐ Post quality images and video
- ☐ Share Blog Posts
- ☐ Share other's content
- ☐ Post Regularly (add at least one new image daily – 2x max)

List 20 Most Used HashTags For Your Niche / Industry

- ☐ Add value
- ☐ Post insightful comments

Instagram Tools

- ☐ Filters – Visual effects over images and videos
- ☐ Video – Upload 3-15 second video directly to Instagram
- ☐ Instagram Workbook and Planner

Instagram Strategy

1. Is my preferred client using Instagram?
2. What is my objective?
3. I have a professional photo or logo on my profile.
4. I have added contact info and URL to profile
5. I have included a keyword rich bio.
6. Use short, SEO descriptions on posts.
7. Add relevant #hashtags to posts.
8. Use #hashtags in comments.
9. Use custom #hashtags on promotions, products, etc.
10. Share Instagram posts on other social media.
11. I am personable, real and authentic.
12. Integrate Instagram on my website
    - ☐ Instagram Profile buttons
    - ☐ Instagram Widget
    - ☐ Embed Instagram posts on blog posts where applicable.
13. I have a (monthly/ weekly / daily) schedule for Instagram.
14. I have a (monthly/ weekly/ daily) Instagram engagement schedule.
    - ☐ Like
    - ☐ Comment
    - ☐ Tag people
    - ☐ Follow and follow back
    - ☐ Respond to comments
15. I have a strategy to capture leads from Instagram.
16. I have a strategy to get fans and friends to buy.
17. I always add value.
18. I am always connecting to:
    - ☐ Influencers and bloggers
    - ☐ Current, Past and Future Clients
    - ☐ Future Collaborators
    - ☐ Family and Friends
    - ☐ Brands

Instagram Status Updates

Instagram Updates	Date	TIme	✓

YouTube

Post Ideas

- ☐ Create a video editorial calendar
- ☐ Reviews, demos, tutorials, testimonials and commercials

List Channels to Subscribe / Start

- ☐ Add value
- ☐ Post insightful comments

YouTube Tools

- ☐ Playlists – Group services, tutorials, client resources, or theme categories
- ☐ G+ Hangouts – Create live broadcasts on YouTube

YouTube Strategy

1. What is my YouTube marketing objective?
2. I included a professional photo on my personal profile.
3. I have a completed YouTube Channel (Icon, Art, Description, Links and URL).
4. I have created branded preview image for each video.
5. I have created a branded video intro and outro.
6. Optimize each video (Keyword in Title, Description, and Tags)
7. Use playlists.
8. Use YouTube Analytics
9. Use annotations – text, links, and graphics placed over video
10. Link to other social media platforms.
11. Integrate YouTube on my website
    - ☐ YouTube Profile buttons
    - ☐ YouTube Widget
    - ☐ YouTube Share buttons
    - ☐ Embed YouTube posts on blog posts.
12. I have a (monthly/ weekly / daily) schedule for YouTube.
13. I have a (monthly/ weekly/ daily) YouTube engagement schedule.
    - ☐ Share videos on other social media channels.
    - ☐ Like, share and comment on others' videos.
    - ☐ Respond to comments.
    - ☐ Subscribe to others' YouTube Channels.
14. I have a strategy to capture leads from YouTube.
15. I have a strategy to get fans and friends to buy.
16. I always add value.
17. I am always connecting to:
    - ☐ Influencers
    - ☐ Current, Past and Future Clients
    - ☐ Future Collaborators
    - ☐ Family and Friends

Campaign Sheet

Product / Service Campaign

Campaign	
Description	
Product / Service Newsletter Contest / Giveaway	
Start	End
Objective	
Target Audience	
Budget$ / Cost$ / Return$	
Landing Page	
Tracking Link	
Days and Time	
Winner / Date Notified	

Image

- ☐ Blog Post Announcement
- ☐ Blog Post Follow-up
- ☐ Autoresponder Setup
- ☐ Ad Campaign
  - Budget$
  - Cost$
  - Return$
  - Click Thru Rate
  - CPC (Cost per Click)
- ☐ Conversion Rate
- ☐ Hashtag
- ☐ Coupon Code (if applicable)

Campaign Sheet

Advertising Campaign

Campaign	
Boost / Ad	
Description	
Start	End
Objective	
Target Audience	
Budget$ / Cost Per Day$	
Landing Page	
Tracking Link	

Text

Demographic

Image

To Do

	Priority	Completed

Notes

Editorial Calendar

Month

SUNDAY	MONDAY	TUESDAY	WEDNESDAY	THURSDAY	FRIDAY	SATURDAY

Notes

Success Tracker

Acknowledge and Celebrate Your Success

Month:

Post with most engagement (shares, likes, and comments) on Facebook	Total Reach This Month
Most retweeted post on Twitter and number of retweets	Number of @Mentions
Most repined post on Pinterest and number of repins	Best Performing Board
Most loved Instagram photo this month and number of loves	Most Successful Hashtag
Most viewed video on YouTube and number of views	Number of videos uploaded this Month

This month I learned

A record I broke this month

My celebration this month

Next month I plan to do the same

Next month I plan to try (new)

Social Media Monthly Stats

FACEBOOK	Total Fans	New Fans	# of Posts	# of Likes	# of Comments	# of Clicks to Website
TWITTER	Total Followers	New Followers	# of Tweets	# of RT's	# of Favorites	# of Clicks to Website
GOOGLE+	Total Followers	New Followers	# of Posts	# of +1's	# of Comments	# of Clicks to Website
PINTEREST	Total Followers	New Followers	# of Pins	# of Repins	# of Likes	# of Clicks to Website
INSTAGRAM	Total Followers	New Followers	# of Pics	# of Comments/Likes		
LINKEDIN	Total Connections	New Connections	# of Posts	# of Comments/Likes		# of Clicks to Website
Other	Total Followers	New Followers	# of Posts	# of Engagement		# of Clicks to Website
EMAIL SUBSCRIBERS FROM SOCIAL MEDIA						

Social Media Posts

	Date	Posts	Post Scheduled	
Mon				
Tue				
Wed				
Thu				
Fri				
Sat				
Sun				
Mon				
Tue				
Wed				
Thu				
Fri				
Sat				
Sun				
Mon				
Tue				
Wed				
Thu				
Fri				
Sat				
Sun				
Mon				
Tue				
Wed				
Thu				
Fri				
Sat				
Sun				

Facebook

Post Ideas

- ☐ Post links, photos, events and video
- ☐ Share Blog Posts in Groups, Status Updates, and Facebook Page
- ☐ Share other's content
- ☐ Post Regularly (max 2 times a day on your page)

List Groups to Join / Start

- ☐ Add value
- ☐ Ask and respond to questions
- ☐ Post insightful comments
- ☐ Announce new members to your group

Facebook Tools

- ☐ Video – uploading video direct to Facebook gets more exposure
- ☐ Photo – create blog posts albums by category
- ☐ Apps / Tabs - Pinterest, Twitter, Instagram, email subscription etc.
- ☐ Facebook Workbook and Planner

Facebook Strategy

1. Is my preferred client using Facebook?
2. What is my objective?
3. Have I included a professional photo on my personal profile?
4. Do I have a completed Facebook Page with a logo, and branded cover?
5. About section includes keywords and URL - reflects my voice and brand.
6. Claim my custom Facebook URL.
7. Use insights to create targeted posts and know the best day and time for engagement.
8. I create super targeted ads with Facebook Advertising.
9. Integrate Facebook on my website
   - ☐ Facebook Profile buttons
   - ☐ Facebook Widget
   - ☐ Facebook Share buttons
   - ☐ Embed Facebook posts on blog posts
10. I have a (monthly/ weekly / daily) schedule for Facebook.
11. I have a (monthly/ weekly/ daily) Facebook engagement schedule.
    - ☐ Post Status Updates and in groups
    - ☐ Respond to all messages and comments on my page
    - ☐ Tag people when I post their content
    - ☐ Comment as my page
12. I have a strategy to capture leads from Facebook.
13. I have a strategy to get fans and friends to buy.
14. I always add value.
15. I am always connecting to:
    - ☐ Influencers
    - ☐ Current, Past and Future Clients
    - ☐ Future Collaborators
    - ☐ Family and Friends

Facebook Status Updates

Facebook Status Updates	Date	TIme	✓

Twitter

Post Ideas

- [ ] Post links, photos, and video
- [ ] Share Blog Posts in Groups, Status Updates and Twitter Page
- [ ] Share other's content
- [ ] Post Regularly

List Twitter Chats To Join / Start

- [ ] Add value
- [ ] Ask and respond to questions
- [ ] Post insightful comments
- [ ] Participate in niche, industry, and interests chats

Twitter Tools

- [ ] Lists – Create public and private lists
- [ ] Images and Video – Post branded photos and videos
- [ ] Twitter Cards – Add twitter cards to your website
- [ ] Twitter Workbook and Planner

Twitter Strategy

1. Is my preferred client using Twitter?
2. What is my objective?
3. Branded Bio, URL, profile image (professional photo or logo) profile header, and background image.
4. Link to other social media profiles
5. Always use #hashtags.
6. Use Twitter Analytics to create targeted posts.
7. Use Twitter Ads.
8. Integrate Twitter on my website

- [ ] Twitter Profile buttons
- [ ] Twitter Widget
- [ ] Twitter Share buttons
- [ ] Embed Twitter posts on blog posts and/or testimonials
- [ ] Use click to Tweet

9. Preface posts with comments
10. Periodically clean up my Twitter feed and unfollow spam and inactive accounts.
11. I have a (monthly/ weekly / daily) schedule for Twitter.
12. I have a (monthly/ weekly/ daily) Twitter engagement schedule.

- [ ] Update
- [ ] Retweet
- [ ] Respond
- [ ] Favorite
- [ ] Mention
- [ ] Direct Message

13. I have a strategy to capture leads from Twitter.
14. I have a strategy to get fans and friends to buy.
15. I always add value.
16. I am always connecting to:

- [ ] Influencers
- [ ] Current, Past and Future Clients
- [ ] Future Collaborators
- [ ] Family and Friends

Twitter Status Updates

Twitter Status Updates	Date	TIme	✓

LinkedIn

Post Ideas

- ☐ Utilize LinkedIn Posts
- ☐ Share Blog Posts in Groups, Status Updates, and Company Page
- ☐ Share other's content
- ☐ Links
- ☐ Post Regularly

List Groups to Join / Start

- ☐ Add value
- ☐ Ask and respond to questions
- ☐ Post insightful comments

LinkedIn Tools

- ☐ Projects – projects you have worked on and completed
- ☐ Publications – books, eBooks, workbooks, planners, etc., you have created
- ☐ Portfolio – showcase your work / creations
- ☐ LinkedIn Workbook and Planner

LinkedIn Strategy

1. Is my preferred client using LinkedIn?
2. What is my objective?
3. Have I included a professional photo?
4. Do I have a branded bio – my voice and brand?
5. Is my profile 100% complete?
6. Is my profile Search Engine Optimized?
7. My posts are compelling content and includes images
8. I have a (monthly/ weekly / daily) schedule for LinkedIn.
9. I have a (monthly/ weekly/ daily) LinkedIn engagement schedule.
   - ☐ Status Updates
   - ☐ Groups
   - ☐ Endorsements
   - ☐ Recommendations
10. I have a completed Company Page.
11. I have a strategy to capture leads from LinkedIn.
12. I have a strategy to get connections and followers to buy.
13. I always add value.
14. I am always connecting to:
    - ☐ Influencers
    - ☐ Current and Past Clients
    - ☐ Future Clients
    - ☐ Future Collaborators
    - ☐ Family and Friends

LinkedIn Status Updates

LinkedIn Status Updates	Date	TIme	✓

Google+

Post Ideas

- ☐ Post texts, links, photos, events, and video
- ☐ Share Blog Posts in Communities, Status Updates and Google+ Page
- ☐ Share other's content
- ☐ Post Regularly

List G+ Communities To Join / Start

- ☐ Add value
- ☐ Ask and respond to questions
- ☐ Post insightful comments at least once a week

Google+ Tools

- ☐ Create Targeted Circles – Influencers, clients, prospects and top engagers
- ☐ G+ Communities – Join communities and follow members
- ☐ Attend and Host G+ Hangouts – Live on air, webinar, panel discussion, video conference, video call, client meetings, screen share, etc
- ☐ Google+ Workbook and Planner

Google+ Strategy

1. Is my preferred client using Google+?
2. What is my objective?
3. Create a G+ profile page, and include professional photo.
4. Create a branded G+ Business Page (Description, Tagline, URL, logo, cover image, contact info, etc.).
5. Claim G+ authorship.
6. Claim your custom URL.
7. Share Google+ posts on other social media profiles.
8. Always use #hashtags.
9. Use keywords and descriptions.
10. Be consistent.
11. Vary posts – long and short
12. Use Google Analytics to create targeted posts.
13. Schedule posts.
14. Integrate Google+ on my website.
    - ☐ Google+ Badge
    - ☐ Google+ Profile buttons
    - ☐ Google+ Share buttons
15. I have a (monthly/ weekly / daily) schedule for Google+.
16. I have a (monthly/ weekly/ daily) Google+ engagement schedule.
    - ☐ +1
    - ☐ Comment
    - ☐ Mention (+ in front of name)
    - ☐ Respond to mentions
    - ☐ Thank people who share my content
    - ☐ Tag people when I share their content
17. I have a strategy to capture leads from Google+.
18. I always add value.
19. I am always connecting to:
    - ☐ Influencers
    - ☐ Current, Past and Future Clients
    - ☐ Future Collaborators
    - ☐ Family and Friends

Google+ Status Updates

Google+ Status Updates	Date	TIme	✓

Pinterest

Post Ideas

- [ ] Share Blog Posts on multiple boards (ensure each blog post has a pinnable image and make more than one image per blog posts)
- [ ] Share other's content
- [ ] Post Regularly

List Group Boards to Join / Start

- [ ] Add value
- [ ] Post insightful comments

Pinterest Tools

- [ ] Boards – Organize and SEO your boards with optimized board names and descriptions
- [ ] Video – Pin branded videos
- [ ] Pinterest Workbook and Planner

Pinterest Strategy

1. Is my preferred client using Pinterest?
2. What is my objective?
3. Have a I included a professional photo or logo in my profile.
4. Get verified and claim your custom Pinterest URL.
5. Use quality images.
6. Schedule posts.
7. Use #hashtags.
8. Vary vertical and horizontal images.
9. Use Pinterest Analytics to see what images people are pinning.
10. Use Pinterest Advertising.
11. Integrate Pinterest on my website

- [ ] Pinterest Profile buttons
- [ ] PinIt button
- [ ] Pinterest Widget
- [ ] Pinterest Share buttons
- [ ] Embed Pinterest boards and posts on blog posts.

12. I have a (monthly/ weekly / daily) schedule for Pinterest.
13. I have a (monthly/ weekly/ daily) Pinterest engagement schedule.

- [ ] Follow users
- [ ] Like
- [ ] Repin
- [ ] Respond to mentions
- [ ] Tag others
- [ ] Comment

14. I have a strategy to capture leads from Pinterest.
15. I have a strategy to get fans and friends to buy.
16. I always add value.
17. I am always connecting to:

- [ ] Influencers
- [ ] Current, Past and Future Clients
- [ ] Future Collaborators
- [ ] Family and Friends

Pinterest Status Updates

Pins	Date	TIme	✓

Instagram

Post Ideas

- ☐ Post quality images and video
- ☐ Share Blog Posts
- ☐ Share other's content
- ☐ Post Regularly (add at least one new image daily – 2x max)

List 20 Most Used HashTags For Your Niche / Industry

- ☐ Add value
- ☐ Post insightful comments

Instagram Tools

- ☐ Filters – Visual effects over images and videos
- ☐ Video – Upload 3-15 second video directly to Instagram
- ☐ Instagram Workbook and Planner

Instagram Strategy

1. Is my preferred client using Instagram?
2. What is my objective?
3. I have a professional photo or logo on my profile.
4. I have added contact info and URL to profile
5. I have included a keyword rich bio.
6. Use short, SEO descriptions on posts.
7. Add relevant #hashtags to posts.
8. Use #hashtags in comments.
9. Use custom #hashtags on promotions, products, etc.
10. Share Instagram posts on other social media.
11. I am personable, real and authentic.
12. Integrate Instagram on my website
    - ☐ Instagram Profile buttons
    - ☐ Instagram Widget
    - ☐ Embed Instagram posts on blog posts where applicable.
13. I have a (monthly/ weekly / daily) schedule for Instagram.
14. I have a (monthly/ weekly/ daily) Instagram engagement schedule.
    - ☐ Like
    - ☐ Comment
    - ☐ Tag people
    - ☐ Follow and follow back
    - ☐ Respond to comments
15. I have a strategy to capture leads from Instagram.
16. I have a strategy to get fans and friends to buy.
17. I always add value.
18. I am always connecting to:
    - ☐ Influencers and bloggers
    - ☐ Current, Past and Future Clients
    - ☐ Future Collaborators
    - ☐ Family and Friends
    - ☐ Brands

Instagram Status Updates

Instagram Updates	Date	TIme	✓

YouTube

Post Ideas

☐ Create a video editorial calendar

☐ Reviews, demos, tutorials, testimonials and commercials

List Channels to Subscribe / Start

☐ Add value

☐ Post insightful comments

YouTube Tools

☐ Playlists – Group services, tutorials, client resources, or theme categories

☐ G+ Hangouts – Create live broadcasts on YouTube

YouTube Strategy

1. What is my YouTube marketing objective?
2. I included a professional photo on my personal profile.
3. I have a completed YouTube Channel (Icon, Art, Description, Links and URL).
4. I have created branded preview image for each video.
5. I have created a branded video intro and outro.
6. Optimize each video (Keyword in Title, Description, and Tags)
7. Use playlists.
8. Use YouTube Analytics
9. Use annotations – text, links, and graphics placed over video
10. Link to other social media platforms.
11. Integrate YouTube on my website

☐ YouTube Profile buttons

☐ YouTube Widget

☐ YouTube Share buttons

☐ Embed YouTube posts on blog posts.

12. I have a (monthly/ weekly / daily) schedule for YouTube.
13. I have a (monthly/ weekly/ daily) YouTube engagement schedule.

☐ Share videos on other social media channels.

☐ Like, share and comment on others' videos.

☐ Respond to comments.

☐ Subscribe to others' YouTube Channels.

14. I have a strategy to capture leads from YouTube.
15. I have a strategy to get fans and friends to buy.
16. I always add value.
17. I am always connecting to:

☐ Influencers

☐ Current, Past and Future Clients

☐ Future Collaborators

☐ Family and Friends

Campaign Sheet

Product / Service Campaign

Campaign	
Description	
Product / Service Newsletter Contest / Giveaway	
Start	End
Objective	
Target Audience	
Budget$ / Cost$ / Return$	
Landing Page	
Tracking Link	
Days and Time	
Winner / Date Notified	

Image

- ☐ Blog Post Announcement
- ☐ Blog Post Follow-up
- ☐ Autoresponder Setup
- ☐ Ad Campaign
  - Budget$
  - Cost$
  - Return$
  - Click Thru Rate
  - CPC (Cost per Click)
- ☐ Conversion Rate
- ☐ Hashtag
- ☐ Coupon Code (if applicable)

Campaign Sheet

Advertising Campaign

Campaign	
Boost / Ad	
Description	
Start	End
Objective	
Target Audience	
Budget$ / Cost Per Day$	
Landing Page	
Tracking Link	

Text

Demographic

Image

To Do

	Priority	Completed

NOTES

Editorial Calendar

Month

SUNDAY	MONDAY	TUESDAY	WEDNESDAY	THURSDAY	FRIDAY	SATURDAY

Notes

ACKNOWLEDGE AND CELEBRATE YOUR SUCCESS

MONTH:

Post with most engagement (shares, likes, and comments) on Facebook	Total Reach This Month
Most retweeted post on Twitter and number of retweets	Number of @Mentions
Most repined post on Pinterest and number of repins	Best Performing Board
Most loved Instagram photo this month and number of loves	Most Successful Hashtag
Most viewed video on YouTube and number of views	Number of videos uploaded this Month

This month I learned

A record I broke this month

My celebration this month

Next month I plan to do the same

Next month I plan to try (new)

Social Media Monthly Stats

FACEBOOK	Total Fans	New Fans	# of Posts	# of Likes	# of Comments	# of Clicks to Website
TWITTER	Total Followers	New Followers	# of Tweets	# of RT's	# of Favorites	# of Clicks to Website
GOOGLE+	Total Followers	New Followers	# of Posts	# of +1's	# of Comments	# of Clicks to Website
PINTEREST	Total Followers	New Followers	# of Pins	# of Repins	# of Likes	# of Clicks to Website
INSTAGRAM	Total Followers	New Followers	# of Pics	# of Comments/Likes		
LINKEDIN	Total Connections	New Connections	# of Posts	# of Comments/Likes		# of Clicks to Website
Other	Total Followers	New Followers	# of Posts	# of Engagement		# of Clicks to Website
EMAIL SUBSCRIBERS FROM SOCIAL MEDIA						

Social Media Posts

	Date	Posts	Post Scheduled	
Mon				
Tue				
Wed				
Thu				
Fri				
Sat				
Sun				
Mon				
Tue				
Wed				
Thu				
Fri				
Sat				
Sun				
Mon				
Tue				
Wed				
Thu				
Fri				
Sat				
Sun				
Mon				
Tue				
Wed				
Thu				
Fri				
Sat				
Sun				

Facebook

Post Ideas

- ☐ Post links, photos, events and video
- ☐ Share Blog Posts in Groups, Status Updates, and Facebook Page
- ☐ Share other's content
- ☐ Post Regularly (max 2 times a day on your page)

List Groups to Join / Start

- ☐ Add value
- ☐ Ask and respond to questions
- ☐ Post insightful comments
- ☐ Announce new members to your group

Facebook Tools

- ☐ Video – uploading video direct to Facebook gets more exposure
- ☐ Photo – create blog posts albums by category
- ☐ Apps / Tabs - Pinterest, Twitter, Instagram, email subscription etc.
- ☐ Facebook Workbook and Planner

Facebook Strategy

1. Is my preferred client using Facebook?
2. What is my objective?
3. Have I included a professional photo on my personal profile?
4. Do I have a completed Facebook Page with a logo, and branded cover?
5. About section includes keywords and URL - reflects my voice and brand.
6. Claim my custom Facebook URL.
7. Use insights to create targeted posts and know the best day and time for engagement.
8. I create super targeted ads with Facebook Advertising.
9. Integrate Facebook on my website
   - ☐ Facebook Profile buttons
   - ☐ Facebook Widget
   - ☐ Facebook Share buttons
   - ☐ Embed Facebook posts on blog posts
10. I have a (monthly/ weekly / daily) schedule for Facebook.
11. I have a (monthly/ weekly/ daily) Facebook engagement schedule.
   - ☐ Post Status Updates and in groups
   - ☐ Respond to all messages and comments on my page
   - ☐ Tag people when I post their content
   - ☐ Comment as my page
12. I have a strategy to capture leads from Facebook.
13. I have a strategy to get fans and friends to buy.
14. I always add value.
15. I am always connecting to:
   - ☐ Influencers
   - ☐ Current, Past and Future Clients
   - ☐ Future Collaborators
   - ☐ Family and Friends

Facebook Status Updates

Facebook Status Updates	Date	TIme	✓

Twitter

Post Ideas

- ☐ Post links, photos, and video
- ☐ Share Blog Posts in Groups, Status Updates and Twitter Page
- ☐ Share other's content
- ☐ Post Regularly

List Twitter Chats To Join / Start

- ☐ Add value
- ☐ Ask and respond to questions
- ☐ Post insightful comments
- ☐ Participate in niche, industry, and interests chats

Twitter Tools

- ☐ Lists – Create public and private lists
- ☐ Images and Video – Post branded photos and videos
- ☐ Twitter Cards – Add twitter cards to your website
- ☐ Twitter Workbook and Planner

Twitter Strategy

1. Is my preferred client using Twitter?
2. What is my objective?
3. Branded Bio, URL, profile image (professional photo or logo) profile header, and background image.
4. Link to other social media profiles
5. Always use #hashtags.
6. Use Twitter Analytics to create targeted posts.
7. Use Twitter Ads.
8. Integrate Twitter on my website

- ☐ Twitter Profile buttons
- ☐ Twitter Widget
- ☐ Twitter Share buttons
- ☐ Embed Twitter posts on blog posts and/or testimonials
- ☐ Use click to Tweet

9. Preface posts with comments
10. Periodically clean up my Twitter feed and unfollow spam and inactive accounts.
11. I have a (monthly/ weekly / daily) schedule for Twitter.
12. I have a (monthly/ weekly/ daily) Twitter engagement schedule.

- ☐ Update
- ☐ Retweet
- ☐ Respond
- ☐ Favorite
- ☐ Mention
- ☐ Direct Message

13. I have a strategy to capture leads from Twitter.
14. I have a strategy to get fans and friends to buy.
15. I always add value.
16. I am always connecting to:

- ☐ Influencers
- ☐ Current, Past and Future Clients
- ☐ Future Collaborators
- ☐ Family and Friends

Twitter Status Updates

Twitter Status Updates	Date	TIme	✓

LinkedIn

Post Ideas

- [ ] Utilize LinkedIn Posts
- [ ] Share Blog Posts in Groups, Status Updates, and Company Page
- [ ] Share other's content
- [ ] Links
- [ ] Post Regularly

List Groups to Join / Start

- [ ] Add value
- [ ] Ask and respond to questions
- [ ] Post insightful comments

LinkedIn Tools

- [ ] Projects – projects you have worked on and completed
- [ ] Publications – books, eBooks, workbooks, planners, etc., you have created
- [ ] Portfolio – showcase your work / creations
- [ ] LinkedIn Workbook and Planner

LinkedIn Strategy

1. Is my preferred client using LinkedIn?
2. What is my objective?
3. Have I included a professional photo?
4. Do I have a branded bio – my voice and brand?
5. Is my profile 100% complete?
6. Is my profile Search Engine Optimized?
7. My posts are compelling content and includes images
8. I have a (monthly/ weekly / daily) schedule for LinkedIn.
9. I have a (monthly/ weekly/ daily) LinkedIn engagement schedule.
    - [ ] Status Updates
    - [ ] Groups
    - [ ] Endorsements
    - [ ] Recommendations
10. I have a completed Company Page.
11. I have a strategy to capture leads from LinkedIn.
12. I have a strategy to get connections and followers to buy.
13. I always add value.
14. I am always connecting to:
    - [ ] Influencers
    - [ ] Current and Past Clients
    - [ ] Future Clients
    - [ ] Future Collaborators
    - [ ] Family and Friends

LinkedIn Status Updates

LinkedIn Status Updates	Date	TIme	✓

Google+

Post Ideas

- ☐ Post texts, links, photos, events, and video
- ☐ Share Blog Posts in Communities, Status Updates and Google+ Page
- ☐ Share other's content
- ☐ Post Regularly

List G+ Communities To Join / Start

- ☐ Add value
- ☐ Ask and respond to questions
- ☐ Post insightful comments at least once a week

Google+ Tools

- ☐ Create Targeted Circles – Influencers, clients, prospects and top engagers
- ☐ G+ Communities – Join communities and follow members
- ☐ Attend and Host G+ Hangouts – Live on air, webinar, panel discussion, video conference, video call, client meetings, screen share, etc
- ☐ Google+ Workbook and Planner

Google+ Strategy

1. Is my preferred client using Google+?
2. What is my objective?
3. Create a G+ profile page, and include professional photo.
4. Create a branded G+ Business Page (Description, Tagline, URL, logo, cover image, contact info, etc.).
5. Claim G+ authorship.
6. Claim your custom URL.
7. Share Google+ posts on other social media profiles.
8. Always use #hashtags.
9. Use keywords and descriptions.
10. Be consistent.
11. Vary posts – long and short
12. Use Google Analytics to create targeted posts.
13. Schedule posts.
14. Integrate Google+ on my website.
    - ☐ Google+ Badge
    - ☐ Google+ Profile buttons
    - ☐ Google+ Share buttons
15. I have a (monthly/ weekly / daily) schedule for Google+.
16. I have a (monthly/ weekly/ daily) Google+ engagement schedule.
    - ☐ +1
    - ☐ Comment
    - ☐ Mention (+ in front of name)
    - ☐ Respond to mentions
    - ☐ Thank people who share my content
    - ☐ Tag people when I share their content
17. I have a strategy to capture leads from Google+.
18. I always add value.
19. I am always connecting to:
    - ☐ Influencers
    - ☐ Current, Past and Future Clients
    - ☐ Future Collaborators
    - ☐ Family and Friends

Google+ Status Updates

Google+ Status Updates	Date	TIme	✓

Pinterest

Post Ideas

- [ ] Share Blog Posts on multiple boards (ensure each blog post has a pinnable image and make more than one image per blog posts)
- [ ] Share other's content
- [ ] Post Regularly

List Group Boards to Join / Start

- [ ] Add value
- [ ] Post insightful comments

Pinterest Tools

- [ ] Boards – Organize and SEO your boards with optimized board names and descriptions
- [ ] Video – Pin branded videos
- [ ] Pinterest Workbook and Planner

Pinterest Strategy

1. Is my preferred client using Pinterest?
2. What is my objective?
3. Have a I included a professional photo or logo in my profile.
4. Get verified and claim your custom Pinterest URL.
5. Use quality images.
6. Schedule posts.
7. Use #hashtags.
8. Vary vertical and horizontal images.
9. Use Pinterest Analytics to see what images people are pinning.
10. Use Pinterest Advertising.
11. Integrate Pinterest on my website
    - [ ] Pinterest Profile buttons
    - [ ] PinIt button
    - [ ] Pinterest Widget
    - [ ] Pinterest Share buttons
    - [ ] Embed Pinterest boards and posts on blog posts.
12. I have a (monthly/ weekly / daily) schedule for Pinterest.
13. I have a (monthly/ weekly/ daily) Pinterest engagement schedule.
    - [ ] Follow users
    - [ ] Like
    - [ ] Repin
    - [ ] Respond to mentions
    - [ ] Tag others
    - [ ] Comment
14. I have a strategy to capture leads from Pinterest.
15. I have a strategy to get fans and friends to buy.
16. I always add value.
17. I am always connecting to:
    - [ ] Influencers
    - [ ] Current, Past and Future Clients
    - [ ] Future Collaborators
    - [ ] Family and Friends

Pinterest Status Updates

Pins	Date	TIme	✓

Instagram

Post Ideas

- ☐ Post quality images and video
- ☐ Share Blog Posts
- ☐ Share other's content
- ☐ Post Regularly (add at least one new image daily – 2x max)

List 20 Most Used HashTags For Your Niche / Industry

- ☐ Add value
- ☐ Post insightful comments

Instagram Tools

- ☐ Filters – Visual effects over images and videos
- ☐ Video – Upload 3-15 second video directly to Instagram
- ☐ Instagram Workbook and Planner

Instagram Strategy

1. Is my preferred client using Instagram?
2. What is my objective?
3. I have a professional photo or logo on my profile.
4. I have added contact info and URL to profile
5. I have included a keyword rich bio.
6. Use short, SEO descriptions on posts.
7. Add relevant #hashtags to posts.
8. Use #hashtags in comments.
9. Use custom #hashtags on promotions, products, etc.
10. Share Instagram posts on other social media.
11. I am personable, real and authentic.
12. Integrate Instagram on my website
    - ☐ Instagram Profile buttons
    - ☐ Instagram Widget
    - ☐ Embed Instagram posts on blog posts where applicable.
13. I have a (monthly/ weekly / daily) schedule for Instagram.
14. I have a (monthly/ weekly/ daily) Instagram engagement schedule.
    - ☐ Like
    - ☐ Comment
    - ☐ Tag people
    - ☐ Follow and follow back
    - ☐ Respond to comments
15. I have a strategy to capture leads from Instagram.
16. I have a strategy to get fans and friends to buy.
17. I always add value.
18. I am always connecting to:
    - ☐ Influencers and bloggers
    - ☐ Current, Past and Future Clients
    - ☐ Future Collaborators
    - ☐ Family and Friends
    - ☐ Brands

Instagram Status Updates

Instagram Updates	Date	TIme	✓

YouTube

Post Ideas

☐ Create a video editorial calendar

☐ Reviews, demos, tutorials, testimonials and commercials

List Channels to Subscribe / Start

☐ Add value

☐ Post insightful comments

YouTube Tools

☐ Playlists – Group services, tutorials, client resources, or theme categories

☐ G+ Hangouts – Create live broadcasts on YouTube

YouTube Strategy

1. What is my YouTube marketing objective?
2. I included a professional photo on my personal profile.
3. I have a completed YouTube Channel (Icon, Art, Description, Links and URL).
4. I have created branded preview image for each video.
5. I have created a branded video intro and outro.
6. Optimize each video (Keyword in Title, Description, and Tags)
7. Use playlists.
8. Use YouTube Analytics
9. Use annotations – text, links, and graphics placed over video
10. Link to other social media platforms.
11. Integrate YouTube on my website

☐ YouTube Profile buttons

☐ YouTube Widget

☐ YouTube Share buttons

☐ Embed YouTube posts on blog posts.

12. I have a (monthly/ weekly / daily) schedule for YouTube.
13. I have a (monthly/ weekly/ daily) YouTube engagement schedule.

☐ Share videos on other social media channels.

☐ Like, share and comment on others' videos.

☐ Respond to comments.

☐ Subscribe to others' YouTube Channels.

14. I have a strategy to capture leads from YouTube.
15. I have a strategy to get fans and friends to buy.
16. I always add value.
17. I am always connecting to:

☐ Influencers

☐ Current, Past and Future Clients

☐ Future Collaborators

☐ Family and Friends

Campaign Sheet

Product / Service Campaign

Campaign	
Description	
Product / Service Newsletter Contest / Giveaway	
Start	End
Objective	
Target Audience	
Budget$ / Cost$ / Return$	
Landing Page	
Tracking Link	
Days and Time	
Winner / Date Notified	

Image

- ☐ Blog Post Announcement
- ☐ Blog Post Follow-up
- ☐ Autoresponder Setup
- ☐ Ad Campaign
  - Budget$
  - Cost$
  - Return$
  - Click Thru Rate
  - CPC (Cost per Click)
- ☐ Conversion Rate
- ☐ Hashtag
- ☐ Coupon Code (if applicable)

Campaign Sheet

Advertising Campaign

Campaign	
Boost / Ad	
Description	
Start	End
Objective	
Target Audience	
Budget$ / Cost Per Day$	
Landing Page	
Tracking Link	

Text

Demographic

Image

To Do

	Priority	Completed

Notes

Editorial Calendar

Month

SUNDAY	MONDAY	TUESDAY	WEDNESDAY	THURSDAY	FRIDAY	SATURDAY

Notes

Acknowledge and Celebrate Your Success

Month:

Post with most engagement (shares, likes, and comments) on Facebook	Total Reach This Month
Most retweeted post on Twitter and number of retweets	Number of @Mentions
Most repined post on Pinterest and number of repins	Best Performing Board
Most loved Instagram photo this month and number of loves	Most Successful Hashtag
Most viewed video on YouTube and number of views	Number of videos uploaded this Month

This month I learned

A record I broke this month

My celebration this month

Next month I plan to do the same

Next month I plan to try (new)

Social Media Monthly Stats

FACEBOOK	Total Fans	New Fans	# of Posts	# of Likes	# of Comments	# of Clicks to Website
TWITTER	Total Followers	New Followers	# of Tweets	# of RT's	# of Favorites	# of Clicks to Website
GOOGLE+	Total Followers	New Followers	# of Posts	# of +1's	# of Comments	# of Clicks to Website
PINTEREST	Total Followers	New Followers	# of Pins	# of Repins	# of Likes	# of Clicks to Website
INSTAGRAM	Total Followers	New Followers	# of Pics	# of Comments/Likes		
LINKEDIN	Total Connections	New Connections	# of Posts	# of Comments/Likes		# of Clicks to Website
Other	Total Followers	New Followers	# of Posts	# of Engagement		# of Clicks to Website
EMAIL SUBSCRIBERS FROM SOCIAL MEDIA						

Social Media Posts

	Date	Posts	Post Scheduled	
Mon				
Tue				
Wed				
Thu				
Fri				
Sat				
Sun				
Mon				
Tue				
Wed				
Thu				
Fri				
Sat				
Sun				
Mon				
Tue				
Wed				
Thu				
Fri				
Sat				
Sun				
Mon				
Tue				
Wed				
Thu				
Fri				
Sat				
Sun				

Facebook

Post Ideas

- ☐ Post links, photos, events and video
- ☐ Share Blog Posts in Groups, Status Updates, and Facebook Page
- ☐ Share other's content
- ☐ Post Regularly (max 2 times a day on your page)

List Groups to Join / Start

- ☐ Add value
- ☐ Ask and respond to questions
- ☐ Post insightful comments
- ☐ Announce new members to your group

Facebook Tools

- ☐ Video – uploading video direct to Facebook gets more exposure
- ☐ Photo – create blog posts albums by category
- ☐ Apps / Tabs - Pinterest, Twitter, Instagram, email subscription etc.
- ☐ Facebook Workbook and Planner

Facebook Strategy

1. Is my preferred client using Facebook?
2. What is my objective?
3. Have I included a professional photo on my personal profile?
4. Do I have a completed Facebook Page with a logo, and branded cover?
5. About section includes keywords and URL - reflects my voice and brand.
6. Claim my custom Facebook URL.
7. Use insights to create targeted posts and know the best day and time for engagement.
8. I create super targeted ads with Facebook Advertising.
9. Integrate Facebook on my website
   - ☐ Facebook Profile buttons
   - ☐ Facebook Widget
   - ☐ Facebook Share buttons
   - ☐ Embed Facebook posts on blog posts
10. I have a (monthly/ weekly / daily) schedule for Facebook.
11. I have a (monthly/ weekly/ daily) Facebook engagement schedule.
   - ☐ Post Status Updates and in groups
   - ☐ Respond to all messages and comments on my page
   - ☐ Tag people when I post their content
   - ☐ Comment as my page
12. I have a strategy to capture leads from Facebook.
13. I have a strategy to get fans and friends to buy.
14. I always add value.
15. I am always connecting to:
   - ☐ Influencers
   - ☐ Current, Past and Future Clients
   - ☐ Future Collaborators
   - ☐ Family and Friends

Facebook Status Updates

Facebook Status Updates	Date	TIme	✓

Twitter

Post Ideas

- ☐ Post links, photos, and video
- ☐ Share Blog Posts in Groups, Status Updates and Twitter Page
- ☐ Share other's content
- ☐ Post Regularly

List Twitter Chats To Join / Start

- ☐ Add value
- ☐ Ask and respond to questions
- ☐ Post insightful comments
- ☐ Participate in niche, industry, and interests chats

Twitter Tools

- ☐ Lists – Create public and private lists
- ☐ Images and Video – Post branded photos and videos
- ☐ Twitter Cards – Add twitter cards to your website
- ☐ Twitter Workbook and Planner

Twitter Strategy

1. Is my preferred client using Twitter?
2. What is my objective?
3. Branded Bio, URL, profile image (professional photo or logo) profile header, and background image.
4. Link to other social media profiles
5. Always use #hashtags.
6. Use Twitter Analytics to create targeted posts.
7. Use Twitter Ads.
8. Integrate Twitter on my website

- ☐ Twitter Profile buttons
- ☐ Twitter Widget
- ☐ Twitter Share buttons
- ☐ Embed Twitter posts on blog posts and/or testimonials
- ☐ Use click to Tweet

9. Preface posts with comments
10. Periodically clean up my Twitter feed and unfollow spam and inactive accounts.
11. I have a (monthly/ weekly / daily) schedule for Twitter.
12. I have a (monthly/ weekly/ daily) Twitter engagement schedule.

- ☐ Update
- ☐ Respond
- ☐ Mention
- ☐ Retweet
- ☐ Favorite
- ☐ Direct Message

13. I have a strategy to capture leads from Twitter.
14. I have a strategy to get fans and friends to buy.
15. I always add value.
16. I am always connecting to:

- ☐ Influencers
- ☐ Current, Past and Future Clients
- ☐ Future Collaborators
- ☐ Family and Friends

Twitter Status Updates

Twitter Status Updates	Date	Time	✓

LinkedIn

Post Ideas

- ☐ Utilize LinkedIn Posts
- ☐ Share Blog Posts in Groups, Status Updates, and Company Page
- ☐ Share other's content
- ☐ Links
- ☐ Post Regularly

List Groups to Join / Start

- ☐ Add value
- ☐ Ask and respond to questions
- ☐ Post insightful comments

LinkedIn Tools

- ☐ Projects – projects you have worked on and completed
- ☐ Publications – books, eBooks, workbooks, planners, etc., you have created
- ☐ Portfolio – showcase your work / creations
- ☐ LinkedIn Workbook and Planner

LinkedIn Strategy

1. Is my preferred client using LinkedIn?
2. What is my objective?
3. Have I included a professional photo?
4. Do I have a branded bio – my voice and brand?
5. Is my profile 100% complete?
6. Is my profile Search Engine Optimized?
7. My posts are compelling content and includes images
8. I have a (monthly/ weekly / daily) schedule for LinkedIn.
9. I have a (monthly/ weekly/ daily) LinkedIn engagement schedule.
   - ☐ Status Updates
   - ☐ Groups
   - ☐ Endorsements
   - ☐ Recommendations
10. I have a completed Company Page.
11. I have a strategy to capture leads from LinkedIn.
12. I have a strategy to get connections and followers to buy.
13. I always add value.
14. I am always connecting to:
    - ☐ Influencers
    - ☐ Current and Past Clients
    - ☐ Future Clients
    - ☐ Future Collaborators
    - ☐ Family and Friends

LinkedIn Status Updates

LinkedIn Status Updates	Date	TIme	✓

Google+

Post Ideas

- ☐ Post texts, links, photos, events, and video
- ☐ Share Blog Posts in Communities, Status Updates and Google+ Page
- ☐ Share other's content
- ☐ Post Regularly

List G+ Communities To Join / Start

- ☐ Add value
- ☐ Ask and respond to questions
- ☐ Post insightful comments at least once a week

Google+ Tools

- ☐ Create Targeted Circles – Influencers, clients, prospects and top engagers
- ☐ G+ Communities – Join communities and follow members
- ☐ Attend and Host G+ Hangouts – Live on air, webinar, panel discussion, video conference, video call, client meetings, screen share, etc
- ☐ Google+ Workbook and Planner

Google+ Strategy

1. Is my preferred client using Google+?
2. What is my objective?
3. Create a G+ profile page, and include professional photo.
4. Create a branded G+ Business Page (Description, Tagline, URL, logo, cover image, contact info, etc.).
5. Claim G+ authorship.
6. Claim your custom URL.
7. Share Google+ posts on other social media profiles.
8. Always use #hashtags.
9. Use keywords and descriptions.
10. Be consistent.
11. Vary posts – long and short
12. Use Google Analytics to create targeted posts.
13. Schedule posts.
14. Integrate Google+ on my website.

- ☐ Google+ Badge
- ☐ Google+ Profile buttons
- ☐ Google+ Share buttons

15. I have a (monthly/ weekly / daily) schedule for Google+.
16. I have a (monthly/ weekly/ daily) Google+ engagement schedule.

- ☐ +1
- ☐ Comment
- ☐ Mention (+ in front of name)
- ☐ Respond to mentions
- ☐ Thank people who share my content
- ☐ Tag people when I share their content

17. I have a strategy to capture leads from Google+.
18. I always add value.
19. I am always connecting to:

- ☐ Influencers
- ☐ Current, Past and Future Clients
- ☐ Future Collaborators
- ☐ Family and Friends

Google+ Status Updates

Google+ Status Updates	Date	TIme	✓

Pinterest

Post Ideas

☐ Share Blog Posts on multiple boards (ensure each blog post has a pinnable image and make more than one image per blog posts)

☐ Share other's content

☐ Post Regularly

List Group Boards to Join / Start

☐ Add value

☐ Post insightful comments

Pinterest Tools

☐ Boards – Organize and SEO your boards with optimized board names and descriptions

☐ Video – Pin branded videos

☐ Pinterest Workbook and Planner

Pinterest Strategy

1. Is my preferred client using Pinterest?
2. What is my objective?
3. Have a I included a professional photo or logo in my profile.
4. Get verified and claim your custom Pinterest URL.
5. Use quality images.
6. Schedule posts.
7. Use #hashtags.
8. Vary vertical and horizontal images.
9. Use Pinterest Analytics to see what images people are pinning.
10. Use Pinterest Advertising.
11. Integrate Pinterest on my website

☐ Pinterest Profile buttons

☐ PinIt button

☐ Pinterest Widget

☐ Pinterest Share buttons

☐ Embed Pinterest boards and posts on blog posts.

12. I have a (monthly/ weekly / daily) schedule for Pinterest.
13. I have a (monthly/ weekly/ daily) Pinterest engagement schedule.

☐ Follow users

☐ Like

☐ Repin

☐ Respond to mentions

☐ Tag others

☐ Comment

14. I have a strategy to capture leads from Pinterest.
15. I have a strategy to get fans and friends to buy.
16. I always add value.
17. I am always connecting to:

☐ Influencers

☐ Current, Past and Future Clients

☐ Future Collaborators

☐ Family and Friends

Pinterest Status Updates

Pins	Date	TIme	✓

Instagram

Post Ideas

☐ Post quality images and video

☐ Share Blog Posts

☐ Share other's content

☐ Post Regularly (add at least one new image daily – 2x max)

List 20 Most Used HashTags For Your Niche / Industry

☐ Add value

☐ Post insightful comments

Instagram Tools

☐ Filters – Visual effects over images and videos

☐ Video – Upload 3-15 second video directly to Instagram

☐ Instagram Workbook and Planner

Instagram Strategy

1. Is my preferred client using Instagram?
2. What is my objective?
3. I have a professional photo or logo on my profile.
4. I have added contact info and URL to profile
5. I have included a keyword rich bio.
6. Use short, SEO descriptions on posts.
7. Add relevant #hashtags to posts.
8. Use #hashtags in comments.
9. Use custom #hashtags on promotions, products, etc.
10. Share Instagram posts on other social media.
11. I am personable, real and authentic.
12. Integrate Instagram on my website

☐ Instagram Profile buttons

☐ Instagram Widget

☐ Embed Instagram posts on blog posts where applicable.

13. I have a (monthly/ weekly / daily) schedule for Instagram.
14. I have a (monthly/ weekly/ daily) Instagram engagement schedule.

☐ Like

☐ Comment

☐ Tag people

☐ Follow and follow back

☐ Respond to comments

15. I have a strategy to capture leads from Instagram.
16. I have a strategy to get fans and friends to buy.
17. I always add value.
18. I am always connecting to:

☐ Influencers and bloggers

☐ Current, Past and Future Clients

☐ Future Collaborators

☐ Family and Friends

☐ Brands

Instagram Status Updates

Instagram Updates	Date	TIme	✓

YouTube

Post Ideas

☐ Create a video editorial calendar

☐ Reviews, demos, tutorials, testimonials and commercials

List Channels to Subscribe / Start

☐ Add value

☐ Post insightful comments

YouTube Tools

☐ Playlists – Group services, tutorials, client resources, or theme categories

☐ G+ Hangouts – Create live broadcasts on YouTube

YouTube Strategy

1. What is my YouTube marketing objective?
2. I included a professional photo on my personal profile.
3. I have a completed YouTube Channel (Icon, Art, Description, Links and URL).
4. I have created branded preview image for each video.
5. I have created a branded video intro and outro.
6. Optimize each video (Keyword in Title, Description, and Tags)
7. Use playlists.
8. Use YouTube Analytics
9. Use annotations – text, links, and graphics placed over video
10. Link to other social media platforms.
11. Integrate YouTube on my website

☐ YouTube Profile buttons

☐ YouTube Widget

☐ YouTube Share buttons

☐ Embed YouTube posts on blog posts.

12. I have a (monthly/ weekly / daily) schedule for YouTube.
13. I have a (monthly/ weekly/ daily) YouTube engagement schedule.

☐ Share videos on other social media channels.

☐ Like, share and comment on others' videos.

☐ Respond to comments.

☐ Subscribe to others' YouTube Channels.

14. I have a strategy to capture leads from YouTube.
15. I have a strategy to get fans and friends to buy.
16. I always add value.
17. I am always connecting to:

☐ Influencers

☐ Current, Past and Future Clients

☐ Future Collaborators

☐ Family and Friends

Campaign Sheet

Product / Service Campaign

Campaign	
Description	
Product / Service Newsletter Contest / Giveaway	
Start	End
Objective	
Target Audience	
Budget$ / Cost$ / Return$	
Landing Page	
Tracking Link	
Days and Time	
Winner / Date Notified	

Image

- ☐ Blog Post Announcement
- ☐ Blog Post Follow-up
- ☐ Autoresponder Setup
- ☐ Ad Campaign
  - Budget$
  - Cost$
  - Return$
  - Click Thru Rate
  - CPC (Cost per Click)
- ☐ Conversion Rate
- ☐ Hashtag
- ☐ Coupon Code (if applicable)

Campaign Sheet

Advertising Campaign

Campaign	
Boost / Ad	
Description	
Start	End
Objective	
Target Audience	
Budget$ / Cost Per Day$	
Landing Page	
Tracking Link	

Text

Demographic

Image

To Do

	Priority	Completed

Notes

Editorial Calendar

Month

SUNDAY	MONDAY	TUESDAY	WEDNESDAY	THURSDAY	FRIDAY	SATURDAY

Notes

Acknowledge and Celebrate Your Success

Month:

Post with most engagement (shares, likes, and comments) on Facebook	Total Reach This Month
Most retweeted post on Twitter and number of retweets	Number of @Mentions
Most repined post on Pinterest and number of repins	Best Performing Board
Most loved Instagram photo this month and number of loves	Most Successful Hashtag
Most viewed video on YouTube and number of views	Number of videos uploaded this Month

This month I learned

A record I broke this month

My celebration this month

Next month I plan to do the same

Next month I plan to try (new)

SOCIAL MEDIA MONTHLY STATS

FACEBOOK	Total Fans	New Fans	# of Posts	# of Likes	# of Comments	# of Clicks to Website
TWITTER	Total Followers	New Followers	# of Tweets	# of RT's	# of Favorites	# of Clicks to Website
GOOGLE+	Total Followers	New Followers	# of Posts	# of +1's	# of Comments	# of Clicks to Website
PINTEREST	Total Followers	New Followers	# of Pins	# of Repins	# of Likes	# of Clicks to Website
INSTAGRAM	Total Followers	New Followers	# of Pics	# of Comments/Likes		
LINKEDIN	Total Connections	New Connections	# of Posts	# of Comments/Likes		# of Clicks to Website
Other	Total Followers	New Followers	# of Posts	# of Engagement		# of Clicks to Website
EMAIL SUBSCRIBERS FROM SOCIAL MEDIA						

Social Media Posts

	Date	Posts	Post Scheduled	
Mon				
Tue				
Wed				
Thu				
Fri				
Sat				
Sun				
Mon				
Tue				
Wed				
Thu				
Fri				
Sat				
Sun				
Mon				
Tue				
Wed				
Thu				
Fri				
Sat				
Sun				
Mon				
Tue				
Wed				
Thu				
Fri				
Sat				
Sun				

Facebook

Post Ideas

- ☐ Post links, photos, events and video
- ☐ Share Blog Posts in Groups, Status Updates, and Facebook Page
- ☐ Share other's content
- ☐ Post Regularly (max 2 times a day on your page)

List Groups to Join / Start

- ☐ Add value
- ☐ Ask and respond to questions
- ☐ Post insightful comments
- ☐ Announce new members to your group

Facebook Tools

- ☐ Video – uploading video direct to Facebook gets more exposure
- ☐ Photo – create blog posts albums by category
- ☐ Apps / Tabs - Pinterest, Twitter, Instagram, email subscription etc.
- ☐ Facebook Workbook and Planner

Facebook Strategy

1. Is my preferred client using Facebook?
2. What is my objective?
3. Have I included a professional photo on my personal profile?
4. Do I have a completed Facebook Page with a logo, and branded cover?
5. About section includes keywords and URL - reflects my voice and brand.
6. Claim my custom Facebook URL.
7. Use insights to create targeted posts and know the best day and time for engagement.
8. I create super targeted ads with Facebook Advertising.
9. Integrate Facebook on my website
   - ☐ Facebook Profile buttons
   - ☐ Facebook Widget
   - ☐ Facebook Share buttons
   - ☐ Embed Facebook posts on blog posts
10. I have a (monthly/ weekly / daily) schedule for Facebook.
11. I have a (monthly/ weekly/ daily) Facebook engagement schedule.
    - ☐ Post Status Updates and in groups
    - ☐ Respond to all messages and comments on my page
    - ☐ Tag people when I post their content
    - ☐ Comment as my page
12. I have a strategy to capture leads from Facebook.
13. I have a strategy to get fans and friends to buy.
14. I always add value.
15. I am always connecting to:
    - ☐ Influencers
    - ☐ Current, Past and Future Clients
    - ☐ Future Collaborators
    - ☐ Family and Friends

Facebook Status Updates

Facebook Status Updates	Date	TIme	✓

Twitter

Post Ideas

- ☐ Post links, photos, and video
- ☐ Share Blog Posts in Groups, Status Updates and Twitter Page
- ☐ Share other's content
- ☐ Post Regularly

List Twitter Chats To Join / Start

- ☐ Add value
- ☐ Ask and respond to questions
- ☐ Post insightful comments
- ☐ Participate in niche, industry, and interests chats

Twitter Tools

- ☐ Lists – Create public and private lists
- ☐ Images and Video – Post branded photos and videos
- ☐ Twitter Cards – Add twitter cards to your website
- ☐ Twitter Workbook and Planner

Twitter Strategy

1. Is my preferred client using Twitter?
2. What is my objective?
3. Branded Bio, URL, profile image (professional photo or logo) profile header, and background image.
4. Link to other social media profiles
5. Always use #hashtags.
6. Use Twitter Analytics to create targeted posts.
7. Use Twitter Ads.
8. Integrate Twitter on my website

- ☐ Twitter Profile buttons
- ☐ Twitter Widget
- ☐ Twitter Share buttons
- ☐ Embed Twitter posts on blog posts and/or testimonials
- ☐ Use click to Tweet

9. Preface posts with comments
10. Periodically clean up my Twitter feed and unfollow spam and inactive accounts.
11. I have a (monthly/ weekly / daily) schedule for Twitter.
12. I have a (monthly/ weekly/ daily) Twitter engagement schedule.

- ☐ Update
- ☐ Retweet
- ☐ Respond
- ☐ Favorite
- ☐ Mention
- ☐ Direct Message

13. I have a strategy to capture leads from Twitter.
14. I have a strategy to get fans and friends to buy.
15. I always add value.
16. I am always connecting to:

- ☐ Influencers
- ☐ Current, Past and Future Clients
- ☐ Future Collaborators
- ☐ Family and Friends

Twitter Status Updates

Twitter Status Updates	Date	TIme	✓

LinkedIn

Post Ideas

- ☐ Utilize LinkedIn Posts
- ☐ Share Blog Posts in Groups, Status Updates, and Company Page
- ☐ Share other's content
- ☐ Links
- ☐ Post Regularly

List Groups to Join / Start

- ☐ Add value
- ☐ Ask and respond to questions
- ☐ Post insightful comments

LinkedIn Tools

- ☐ Projects – projects you have worked on and completed
- ☐ Publications – books, eBooks, workbooks, planners, etc., you have created
- ☐ Portfolio – showcase your work / creations
- ☐ LinkedIn Workbook and Planner

LinkedIn Strategy

1. Is my preferred client using LinkedIn?
2. What is my objective?
3. Have I included a professional photo?
4. Do I have a branded bio – my voice and brand?
5. Is my profile 100% complete?
6. Is my profile Search Engine Optimized?
7. My posts are compelling content and includes images
8. I have a (monthly/ weekly / daily) schedule for LinkedIn.
9. I have a (monthly/ weekly/ daily) LinkedIn engagement schedule.
   - ☐ Status Updates
   - ☐ Groups
   - ☐ Endorsements
   - ☐ Recommendations
10. I have a completed Company Page.
11. I have a strategy to capture leads from LinkedIn.
12. I have a strategy to get connections and followers to buy.
13. I always add value.
14. I am always connecting to:
    - ☐ Influencers
    - ☐ Current and Past Clients
    - ☐ Future Clients
    - ☐ Future Collaborators
    - ☐ Family and Friends

LinkedIn Status Updates

LinkedIn Status Updates	Date	TIme	✓

Google+

Post Ideas

- [ ] Post texts, links, photos, events, and video
- [ ] Share Blog Posts in Communities, Status Updates and Google+ Page
- [ ] Share other's content
- [ ] Post Regularly

List G+ Communities To Join / Start

- [ ] Add value
- [ ] Ask and respond to questions
- [ ] Post insightful comments at least once a week

Google+ Tools

- [ ] Create Targeted Circles – Influencers, clients, prospects and top engagers
- [ ] G+ Communities – Join communities and follow members
- [ ] Attend and Host G+ Hangouts – Live on air, webinar, panel discussion, video conference, video call, client meetings, screen share, etc
- [ ] Google+ Workbook and Planner

Google+ Strategy

1. Is my preferred client using Google+?
2. What is my objective?
3. Create a G+ profile page, and include professional photo.
4. Create a branded G+ Business Page (Description, Tagline, URL, logo, cover image, contact info, etc.).
5. Claim G+ authorship.
6. Claim your custom URL.
7. Share Google+ posts on other social media profiles.
8. Always use #hashtags.
9. Use keywords and descriptions.
10. Be consistent.
11. Vary posts – long and short
12. Use Google Analytics to create targeted posts.
13. Schedule posts.
14. Integrate Google+ on my website.
    - [ ] Google+ Badge
    - [ ] Google+ Profile buttons
    - [ ] Google+ Share buttons
15. I have a (monthly/ weekly / daily) schedule for Google+.
16. I have a (monthly/ weekly/ daily) Google+ engagement schedule.
    - [ ] +1
    - [ ] Comment
    - [ ] Mention (+ in front of name)
    - [ ] Respond to mentions
    - [ ] Thank people who share my content
    - [ ] Tag people when I share their content
17. I have a strategy to capture leads from Google+.
18. I always add value.
19. I am always connecting to:
    - [ ] Influencers
    - [ ] Current, Past and Future Clients
    - [ ] Future Collaborators
    - [ ] Family and Friends

Google+ Status Updates

Google+ Status Updates	Date	TIme	✓

Pinterest

Post Ideas

- ☐ Share Blog Posts on multiple boards (ensure each blog post has a pinnable image and make more than one image per blog posts)
- ☐ Share other's content
- ☐ Post Regularly

List Group Boards to Join / Start

- ☐ Add value
- ☐ Post insightful comments

Pinterest Tools

- ☐ Boards – Organize and SEO your boards with optimized board names and descriptions
- ☐ Video – Pin branded videos
- ☐ Pinterest Workbook and Planner

Pinterest Strategy

1. Is my preferred client using Pinterest?
2. What is my objective?
3. Have a I included a professional photo or logo in my profile.
4. Get verified and claim your custom Pinterest URL.
5. Use quality images.
6. Schedule posts.
7. Use #hashtags.
8. Vary vertical and horizontal images.
9. Use Pinterest Analytics to see what images people are pinning.
10. Use Pinterest Advertising.
11. Integrate Pinterest on my website
    - ☐ Pinterest Profile buttons
    - ☐ PinIt button
    - ☐ Pinterest Widget
    - ☐ Pinterest Share buttons
    - ☐ Embed Pinterest boards and posts on blog posts.
12. I have a (monthly/ weekly / daily) schedule for Pinterest.
13. I have a (monthly/ weekly/ daily) Pinterest engagement schedule.
    - ☐ Follow users
    - ☐ Like
    - ☐ Repin
    - ☐ Respond to mentions
    - ☐ Tag others
    - ☐ Comment
14. I have a strategy to capture leads from Pinterest.
15. I have a strategy to get fans and friends to buy.
16. I always add value.
17. I am always connecting to:
    - ☐ Influencers
    - ☐ Current, Past and Future Clients
    - ☐ Future Collaborators
    - ☐ Family and Friends

Pinterest Status Updates

Pins	Date	TIme	✓

Instagram

Post Ideas

☐ Post quality images and video

☐ Share Blog Posts

☐ Share other's content

☐ Post Regularly (add at least one new image daily – 2x max)

List 20 Most Used HashTags For Your Niche / Industry

☐ Add value

☐ Post insightful comments

Instagram Tools

☐ Filters – Visual effects over images and videos

☐ Video – Upload 3-15 second video directly to Instagram

☐ Instagram Workbook and Planner

Instagram Strategy

1. Is my preferred client using Instagram?
2. What is my objective?
3. I have a professional photo or logo on my profile.
4. I have added contact info and URL to profile
5. I have included a keyword rich bio.
6. Use short, SEO descriptions on posts.
7. Add relevant #hashtags to posts.
8. Use #hashtags in comments.
9. Use custom #hashtags on promotions, products, etc.
10. Share Instagram posts on other social media.
11. I am personable, real and authentic.
12. Integrate Instagram on my website

☐ Instagram Profile buttons

☐ Instagram Widget

☐ Embed Instagram posts on blog posts where applicable.

13. I have a (monthly/ weekly / daily) schedule for Instagram.
14. I have a (monthly/ weekly/ daily) Instagram engagement schedule.

☐ Like

☐ Comment

☐ Tag people

☐ Follow and follow back

☐ Respond to comments

15. I have a strategy to capture leads from Instagram.
16. I have a strategy to get fans and friends to buy.
17. I always add value.
18. I am always connecting to:

☐ Influencers and bloggers

☐ Current, Past and Future Clients

☐ Future Collaborators

☐ Family and Friends

☐ Brands

Instagram Status Updates

Instagram Updates	Date	TIme	✓

YouTube

Post Ideas

- ☐ Create a video editorial calendar
- ☐ Reviews, demos, tutorials, testimonials and commercials

List Channels to Subscribe / Start

- ☐ Add value
- ☐ Post insightful comments

YouTube Tools

- ☐ Playlists – Group services, tutorials, client resources, or theme categories
- ☐ G+ Hangouts – Create live broadcasts on YouTube

YouTube Strategy

1. What is my YouTube marketing objective?
2. I included a professional photo on my personal profile.
3. I have a completed YouTube Channel (Icon, Art, Description, Links and URL).
4. I have created branded preview image for each video.
5. I have created a branded video intro and outro.
6. Optimize each video (Keyword in Title, Description, and Tags)
7. Use playlists.
8. Use YouTube Analytics
9. Use annotations – text, links, and graphics placed over video
10. Link to other social media platforms.
11. Integrate YouTube on my website
    - ☐ YouTube Profile buttons
    - ☐ YouTube Widget
    - ☐ YouTube Share buttons
    - ☐ Embed YouTube posts on blog posts.
12. I have a (monthly/ weekly / daily) schedule for YouTube.
13. I have a (monthly/ weekly/ daily) YouTube engagement schedule.
    - ☐ Share videos on other social media channels.
    - ☐ Like, share and comment on others' videos.
    - ☐ Respond to comments.
    - ☐ Subscribe to others' YouTube Channels.
14. I have a strategy to capture leads from YouTube.
15. I have a strategy to get fans and friends to buy.
16. I always add value.
17. I am always connecting to:
    - ☐ Influencers
    - ☐ Current, Past and Future Clients
    - ☐ Future Collaborators
    - ☐ Family and Friends

Campaign Sheet

Product / Service Campaign

Campaign	
Description	
Product / Service Newsletter Contest / Giveaway	
Start	End
Objective	
Target Audience	
Budget$ / Cost$ / Return$	
Landing Page	
Tracking Link	
Days and Time	
Winner / Date Notified	

Image

- ☐ Blog Post Announcement
- ☐ Blog Post Follow-up
- ☐ Autoresponder Setup
- ☐ Ad Campaign
  - ○ Budget$
  - ○ Cost$
  - ○ Return$
  - ○ Click Thru Rate
  - ○ CPC (Cost per Click)
- ☐ Conversion Rate
- ☐ Hashtag
- ☐ Coupon Code (if applicable)

Campaign Sheet

Advertising Campaign

Campaign	
Boost / Ad	
Description	
Start	End
Objective	
Target Audience	
Budget$ / Cost Per Day$	
Landing Page	
Tracking Link	

Text

Demographic

Image

To Do

	Priority	Completed

Notes

Editorial Calendar

Month

SUNDAY	MONDAY	TUESDAY	WEDNESDAY	THURSDAY	FRIDAY	SATURDAY

Notes

SUCCESS TRACKER

ACKNOWLEDGE AND CELEBRATE YOUR SUCCESS

MONTH:

Post with most engagement (shares, likes, and comments) on Facebook	Total Reach This Month
Most retweeted post on Twitter and number of retweets	Number of @Mentions
Most repined post on Pinterest and number of repins	Best Performing Board
Most loved Instagram photo this month and number of loves	Most Successful Hashtag
Most viewed video on YouTube and number of views	Number of videos uploaded this Month

This month I learned

A record I broke this month

My celebration this month

Next month I plan to do the same

Next month I plan to try (new)

Social Media Monthly Stats

FACEBOOK	Total Fans	New Fans	# of Posts	# of Likes	# of Comments	# of Clicks to Website
TWITTER	Total Followers	New Followers	# of Tweets	# of RT's	# of Favorites	# of Clicks to Website
GOOGLE+	Total Followers	New Followers	# of Posts	# of +1's	# of Comments	# of Clicks to Website
PINTEREST	Total Followers	New Followers	# of Pins	# of Repins	# of Likes	# of Clicks to Website
INSTAGRAM	Total Followers	New Followers	# of Pics	# of Comments/Likes		
LINKEDIN	Total Connections	New Connections	# of Posts	# of Comments/Likes		# of Clicks to Website
Other	Total Followers	New Followers	# of Posts	# of Engagement		# of Clicks to Website
EMAIL SUBSCRIBERS FROM SOCIAL MEDIA						

Social Media Posts

	Date	Posts	Post Scheduled	
Mon				
Tue				
Wed				
Thu				
Fri				
Sat				
Sun				
Mon				
Tue				
Wed				
Thu				
Fri				
Sat				
Sun				
Mon				
Tue				
Wed				
Thu				
Fri				
Sat				
Sun				
Mon				
Tue				
Wed				
Thu				
Fri				
Sat				
Sun				

Facebook

Post Ideas

- ☐ Post links, photos, events and video
- ☐ Share Blog Posts in Groups, Status Updates, and Facebook Page
- ☐ Share other's content
- ☐ Post Regularly (max 2 times a day on your page)

List Groups to Join / Start

- ☐ Add value
- ☐ Ask and respond to questions
- ☐ Post insightful comments
- ☐ Announce new members to your group

Facebook Tools

- ☐ Video – uploading video direct to Facebook gets more exposure
- ☐ Photo – create blog posts albums by category
- ☐ Apps / Tabs - Pinterest, Twitter, Instagram, email subscription etc.
- ☐ Facebook Workbook and Planner

Facebook Strategy

1. Is my preferred client using Facebook?
2. What is my objective?
3. Have I included a professional photo on my personal profile?
4. Do I have a completed Facebook Page with a logo, and branded cover?
5. About section includes keywords and URL - reflects my voice and brand.
6. Claim my custom Facebook URL.
7. Use insights to create targeted posts and know the best day and time for engagement.
8. I create super targeted ads with Facebook Advertising.
9. Integrate Facebook on my website

- ☐ Facebook Profile buttons
- ☐ Facebook Widget
- ☐ Facebook Share buttons
- ☐ Embed Facebook posts on blog posts

10. I have a (monthly/ weekly / daily) schedule for Facebook.
11. I have a (monthly/ weekly/ daily) Facebook engagement schedule.

- ☐ Post Status Updates and in groups
- ☐ Respond to all messages and comments on my page
- ☐ Tag people when I post their content
- ☐ Comment as my page

12. I have a strategy to capture leads from Facebook.
13. I have a strategy to get fans and friends to buy.
14. I always add value.
15. I am always connecting to:

- ☐ Influencers
- ☐ Current, Past and Future Clients
- ☐ Future Collaborators
- ☐ Family and Friends

Facebook Status Updates

Facebook Status Updates	Date	TIme	✓

Twitter

Post Ideas

- ☐ Post links, photos, and video
- ☐ Share Blog Posts in Groups, Status Updates and Twitter Page
- ☐ Share other's content
- ☐ Post Regularly

List Twitter Chats To Join / Start

- ☐ Add value
- ☐ Ask and respond to questions
- ☐ Post insightful comments
- ☐ Participate in niche, industry, and interests chats

Twitter Tools

- ☐ Lists – Create public and private lists
- ☐ Images and Video – Post branded photos and videos
- ☐ Twitter Cards – Add twitter cards to your website
- ☐ Twitter Workbook and Planner

Twitter Strategy

1. Is my preferred client using Twitter?
2. What is my objective?
3. Branded Bio, URL, profile image (professional photo or logo) profile header, and background image.
4. Link to other social media profiles
5. Always use #hashtags.
6. Use Twitter Analytics to create targeted posts.
7. Use Twitter Ads.
8. Integrate Twitter on my website

- ☐ Twitter Profile buttons
- ☐ Twitter Widget
- ☐ Twitter Share buttons
- ☐ Embed Twitter posts on blog posts and/or testimonials
- ☐ Use click to Tweet

9. Preface posts with comments
10. Periodically clean up my Twitter feed and unfollow spam and inactive accounts.
11. I have a (monthly/ weekly / daily) schedule for Twitter.
12. I have a (monthly/ weekly/ daily) Twitter engagement schedule.

- ☐ Update
- ☐ Retweet
- ☐ Respond
- ☐ Favorite
- ☐ Mention
- ☐ Direct Message

13. I have a strategy to capture leads from Twitter.
14. I have a strategy to get fans and friends to buy.
15. I always add value.
16. I am always connecting to:

- ☐ Influencers
- ☐ Current, Past and Future Clients
- ☐ Future Collaborators
- ☐ Family and Friends

Twitter Status Updates

Twitter Status Updates	Date	TIme	✓

LinkedIn

Post Ideas

- ☐ Utilize LinkedIn Posts
- ☐ Share Blog Posts in Groups, Status Updates, and Company Page
- ☐ Share other's content
- ☐ Links
- ☐ Post Regularly

List Groups to Join / Start

- ☐ Add value
- ☐ Ask and respond to questions
- ☐ Post insightful comments

LinkedIn Tools

- ☐ Projects – projects you have worked on and completed
- ☐ Publications – books, eBooks, workbooks, planners, etc., you have created
- ☐ Portfolio – showcase your work / creations
- ☐ LinkedIn Workbook and Planner

LinkedIn Strategy

1. Is my preferred client using LinkedIn?
2. What is my objective?
3. Have I included a professional photo?
4. Do I have a branded bio – my voice and brand?
5. Is my profile 100% complete?
6. Is my profile Search Engine Optimized?
7. My posts are compelling content and includes images
8. I have a (monthly/ weekly / daily) schedule for LinkedIn.
9. I have a (monthly/ weekly/ daily) LinkedIn engagement schedule.
   - ☐ Status Updates
   - ☐ Groups
   - ☐ Endorsements
   - ☐ Recommendations
10. I have a completed Company Page.
11. I have a strategy to capture leads from LinkedIn.
12. I have a strategy to get connections and followers to buy.
13. I always add value.
14. I am always connecting to:
    - ☐ Influencers
    - ☐ Current and Past Clients
    - ☐ Future Clients
    - ☐ Future Collaborators
    - ☐ Family and Friends

LinkedIn Status Updates

LinkedIn Status Updates	Date	TIme	✓

GOOGLE+

POST IDEAS

- ☐ Post texts, links, photos, events, and video
- ☐ Share Blog Posts in Communities, Status Updates and Google+ Page
- ☐ Share other's content
- ☐ Post Regularly

LIST G+ COMMUNITIES TO JOIN / START

- ☐ Add value
- ☐ Ask and respond to questions
- ☐ Post insightful comments at least once a week

GOOGLE+ TOOLS

- ☐ Create Targeted Circles – Influencers, clients, prospects and top engagers
- ☐ G+ Communities – Join communities and follow members
- ☐ Attend and Host G+ Hangouts – Live on air, webinar, panel discussion, video conference, video call, client meetings, screen share, etc
- ☐ Google+ Workbook and Planner

GOOGLE+ STRATEGY

1. Is my preferred client using Google+?
2. What is my objective?
3. Create a G+ profile page, and include professional photo.
4. Create a branded G+ Business Page (Description, Tagline, URL, logo, cover image, contact info, etc.).
5. Claim G+ authorship.
6. Claim your custom URL.
7. Share Google+ posts on other social media profiles.
8. Always use #hashtags.
9. Use keywords and descriptions.
10. Be consistent.
11. Vary posts – long and short
12. Use Google Analytics to create targeted posts.
13. Schedule posts.
14. Integrate Google+ on my website.
    - ☐ Google+ Badge
    - ☐ Google+ Profile buttons
    - ☐ Google+ Share buttons
15. I have a (monthly/ weekly / daily) schedule for Google+.
16. I have a (monthly/ weekly/ daily) Google+ engagement schedule.
    - ☐ +1
    - ☐ Comment
    - ☐ Mention (+ in front of name)
    - ☐ Respond to mentions
    - ☐ Thank people who share my content
    - ☐ Tag people when I share their content
17. I have a strategy to capture leads from Google+.
18. I always add value.
19. I am always connecting to:
    - ☐ Influencers
    - ☐ Current, Past and Future Clients
    - ☐ Future Collaborators
    - ☐ Family and Friends

Google+ Status Updates

Google+ Status Updates	Date	TIme	✓

Pinterest

Post Ideas

- ☐ Share Blog Posts on multiple boards (ensure each blog post has a pinnable image and make more than one image per blog posts)
- ☐ Share other's content
- ☐ Post Regularly

List Group Boards to Join / Start

- ☐ Add value
- ☐ Post insightful comments

Pinterest Tools

- ☐ Boards – Organize and SEO your boards with optimized board names and descriptions
- ☐ Video – Pin branded videos
- ☐ Pinterest Workbook and Planner

Pinterest Strategy

1. Is my preferred client using Pinterest?
2. What is my objective?
3. Have a I included a professional photo or logo in my profile.
4. Get verified and claim your custom Pinterest URL.
5. Use quality images.
6. Schedule posts.
7. Use #hashtags.
8. Vary vertical and horizontal images.
9. Use Pinterest Analytics to see what images people are pinning.
10. Use Pinterest Advertising.
11. Integrate Pinterest on my website

- ☐ Pinterest Profile buttons
- ☐ PinIt button
- ☐ Pinterest Widget
- ☐ Pinterest Share buttons
- ☐ Embed Pinterest boards and posts on blog posts.

12. I have a (monthly/ weekly / daily) schedule for Pinterest.
13. I have a (monthly/ weekly/ daily) Pinterest engagement schedule.

- ☐ Follow users
- ☐ Like
- ☐ Repin
- ☐ Respond to mentions
- ☐ Tag others
- ☐ Comment

14. I have a strategy to capture leads from Pinterest.
15. I have a strategy to get fans and friends to buy.
16. I always add value.
17. I am always connecting to:

- ☐ Influencers
- ☐ Current, Past and Future Clients
- ☐ Future Collaborators
- ☐ Family and Friends

Pinterest Status Updates

Pins	Date	TIme	✓

Instagram

Post Ideas

- ☐ Post quality images and video
- ☐ Share Blog Posts
- ☐ Share other's content
- ☐ Post Regularly (add at least one new image daily – 2x max)

List 20 Most Used HashTags For Your Niche / Industry

- ☐ Add value
- ☐ Post insightful comments

Instagram Tools

- ☐ Filters – Visual effects over images and videos
- ☐ Video – Upload 3-15 second video directly to Instagram
- ☐ Instagram Workbook and Planner

Instagram Strategy

1. Is my preferred client using Instagram?
2. What is my objective?
3. I have a professional photo or logo on my profile.
4. I have added contact info and URL to profile
5. I have included a keyword rich bio.
6. Use short, SEO descriptions on posts.
7. Add relevant #hashtags to posts.
8. Use #hashtags in comments.
9. Use custom #hashtags on promotions, products, etc.
10. Share Instagram posts on other social media.
11. I am personable, real and authentic.
12. Integrate Instagram on my website

- ☐ Instagram Profile buttons
- ☐ Instagram Widget
- ☐ Embed Instagram posts on blog posts where applicable.

13. I have a (monthly/ weekly / daily) schedule for Instagram.
14. I have a (monthly/ weekly/ daily) Instagram engagement schedule.

- ☐ Like
- ☐ Comment
- ☐ Tag people
- ☐ Follow and follow back
- ☐ Respond to comments

15. I have a strategy to capture leads from Instagram.
16. I have a strategy to get fans and friends to buy.
17. I always add value.
18. I am always connecting to:

- ☐ Influencers and bloggers
- ☐ Current, Past and Future Clients
- ☐ Future Collaborators
- ☐ Family and Friends
- ☐ Brands

Instagram Status Updates

Instagram Updates	Date	TIme	✓

YouTube

Post Ideas

☐ Create a video editorial calendar

☐ Reviews, demos, tutorials, testimonials and commercials

List Channels to Subscribe / Start

☐ Add value

☐ Post insightful comments

YouTube Tools

☐ Playlists – Group services, tutorials, client resources, or theme categories

☐ G+ Hangouts – Create live broadcasts on YouTube

YouTube Strategy

1. What is my YouTube marketing objective?
2. I included a professional photo on my personal profile.
3. I have a completed YouTube Channel (Icon, Art, Description, Links and URL).
4. I have created branded preview image for each video.
5. I have created a branded video intro and outro.
6. Optimize each video (Keyword in Title, Description, and Tags)
7. Use playlists.
8. Use YouTube Analytics
9. Use annotations – text, links, and graphics placed over video
10. Link to other social media platforms.
11. Integrate YouTube on my website

☐ YouTube Profile buttons

☐ YouTube Widget

☐ YouTube Share buttons

☐ Embed YouTube posts on blog posts.

12. I have a (monthly/ weekly / daily) schedule for YouTube.
13. I have a (monthly/ weekly/ daily) YouTube engagement schedule.

☐ Share videos on other social media channels.

☐ Like, share and comment on others' videos.

☐ Respond to comments.

☐ Subscribe to others' YouTube Channels.

14. I have a strategy to capture leads from YouTube.
15. I have a strategy to get fans and friends to buy.
16. I always add value.
17. I am always connecting to:

☐ Influencers

☐ Current, Past and Future Clients

☐ Future Collaborators

☐ Family and Friends

Campaign Sheet

Product / Service Campaign

Campaign	
Description	
Product / Service Newsletter Contest / Giveaway	
Start	End
Objective	
Target Audience	
Budget$ / Cost$ / Return$	
Landing Page	
Tracking Link	
Days and Time	
Winner / Date Notified	

Image

- ☐ Blog Post Announcement
- ☐ Blog Post Follow-up
- ☐ Autoresponder Setup
- ☐ Ad Campaign
  - Budget$
  - Cost$
  - Return$
  - Click Thru Rate
  - CPC (Cost per Click)
- ☐ Conversion Rate
- ☐ Hashtag
- ☐ Coupon Code (if applicable)

Campaign Sheet

Advertising Campaign

Campaign	
Boost / Ad	
Description	
Start	End
Objective	
Target Audience	
Budget$ / Cost Per Day$	
Landing Page	
Tracking Link	

Text

Demographic

Image

To Do

	Priority	Completed

Notes

Thank You

HOPE YOU ENJOYED USING
YOUR SOCIAL MEDIA WORKBOOK AND PLANNER

GET YOUR FREE WEEKLY SOCIAL MEDIA PLANNER!
http://bit.ly/socialmarketingweekly

PLEASE LEAVE A REVIEW ON AMAZON

BE SURE TO GRAB YOUR COPIES
- Facebook Media Marketing Workbook -
- Google+ Workbook and Planner -
- LinkedIn Workbook and Planner -
- Twitter Workbook and Planner -
- Pinterest Workbook and Planner -
- Instagram Workbook and Planner -

ALSO LOOK OUT FOR
Authentic Marketing – The Three E's of Online Marketing: Ethical, Effortless, Engaging
Social Media Marketing: How to Master Engagement in 15 Minutes a Day.

Connect with Dwainia Grey on LinkedIn, Google+, Facebook, Twitter, Pinterest and Instagram
dwainiagrey.me

Made in United States
Orlando, FL
05 November 2026

90231067R00166